THE SELF-DRIVING YOU

THE SELF-DRIVING YOU

Awaken the Driver Within to Rewire Your Brain and Transform Your Life

Alan Bodnar

Published by The Self-Driving You Press
Canada

ISBN 978-1-0699831-3-8 (paperback)
ISBN 978-1-0699831-0-7 (hardcover)
ISBN 978-1-0699831-1-4 (ebook)

Cover design by Jennifer Dunaj

www.theselfdrivingyou.com

For Mallory

Contents

THE SELF-DRIVING YOU

INTRODUCTION

The Self-Driving You

Imagine being behind the wheel of a brand-new Level 4 high-automation self-driving car sometime in the near future. It's not fully autonomous, but it will manage around 80-95 percent of the driving on its own. We're in the driver's seat, playing the role of a supervisor who oversees the vehicle and takes control when needed, the rest of the time.

The self-driving car and the driver work together to navigate the roadway safely. Under normal conditions, we'll sit back with our hands at our sides while the car drives itself. As the driver, we only step in when the vehicle is stuck or if we simply want to drive.

While driving, the car takes in information from its sensors, automatically adjusting the steering wheel, gas, and brakes based on what it processes. As the driver, we cannot control its initial response, but we feel the result of every decision it makes. The vehicle uses an artificial network, trained through experience, to drive independently. The network starts with a goal of navigating the roadway safely and a way to measure success against that goal. From there, it bumps into the environment, learning through trial and error until it shapes a network that can drive on its own.

The human body uses a similar design, relying on an automatic self-driving system to handle up to 95 percent of driving, with a conscious driver to supervise and step in when needed. Our self-driving system provides an initial response to everything we encounter, using survival, intuitive, and default mode circuits that fire outside driver awareness.

These circuits are wiring templates installed at birth that we shape over a lifetime of experience into the automatic responses that drive us. Similar to a self-driving car, the human vehicle has an equivalent sympathetic "gas" and parasympathetic "brake" that our self-driving system uses to carry out its decisions. As the driver, we experience the result of these responses but can only intervene as they happen, if at all.

Fortunately, the brain has executive circuitry that gives rise to the conscious driver at the wheel who can monitor the self-driving system and take corrective action when necessary. Throughout our early life, the driver closely supervises our vehicle's decisions, helping wire the automatic system that will drive us. In adulthood, we sit back and relax, trusting the network we wired to drive itself.

For most, early experiences unknowingly wire our self-driving vehicle to accelerate chronically, while we do our best to hang on. Because the driver helps wire our self-driving responses, they come to view them as accurate, and sleep at the wheel, trusting our vehicle to navigate on its own with minimal supervision.

At any moment, we can engage our driver to override the self-driving system in corrective action, but we don't know how. Deliberate attention is the secret power that allows us to take control of our vehicle with our driver and steer it in the direction we want. With repetition, continually correcting the self-driving system can train it to drive more effectively. Strategically using deliberate attention, especially with practices like mindfulness, is the answer for rewiring our vehicle to drive with greater balance.

Over a decade ago, I was an unsatisfied underachiever with low self-worth, seeking to understand what it means to be human and how to make the most of it. I began listening to an audiobook a week, treating myself as the ultimate test subject, while I applied all the lessons learned to my life in an attempt to find the answer. More than 10,000 hours of research and effort led to this framework for understanding the human vehicle through science and the self-driving metaphor. It shows how deliberate attention is our secret power for wiring our vehicle toward success and well-being.

The first part gets right into the self-driving metaphor, explaining the human vehicle and how we can engage our driver to deliberately wire it in a way that serves us. The second part is more foundational, uncovering the brain as an impartial plastic network that anyone can tune to mastery with 10,000 hours of deliberate practice, regardless of age, sex, race, or social standing.

This book is a starting point meant to provide the information we need to wake up our driver within and rewire our vehicle. It accounts for only 1 percent of our journey toward self-mastery; the other 99 percent is consistently applying it to our lives for thousands of hours as we strengthen our driver within and deliberately use it to rewire our self-driving system in ways that serve us. Buckle your seat belts as we lay out the framework for taking the wheel with our driver and embark on the journey of rewiring our self-driving system to drive with greater balance.

PART 1

The Self-Driving You

CHAPTER 1

Self-Driving Cars

Imagine getting into a driverless taxi sometime in the future. There will be no wheel or gas pedal, only passenger seats, as the car drives itself. Once an idea straight out of a page from a science fiction novel, self-driving vehicles are now becoming a reality.

Many people are hesitant to ride in a fully automatic self-driving car, with about 73 percent of Americans saying they would be afraid.[1] The truth is, we're not very good at driving ourselves, but we've become so accustomed to it that we accept the risk. Globally, there are a million fatalities and fifty million injuries each year related to automobile collisions.[2]

Experts estimate that driverless cars would reduce car accidents by 90 percent.[3] Humans are flawed; we get tired, our attention drifts, and we can be aggressive. A driverless car would respond faster, never tire, and would be less forceful.[4] It will take some getting used to, but after a few trips, we'll let our guard down, and eventually, driverless cars may be all we know. Some experts even suggest that one day the conversation may shift to whether humans should be allowed to drive at all.[5]

Inspired by human nature, AI takes a learning network, gives it a goal, and a way to measure success. From there, it's fed data and, through experience, forms a model of understanding.[6] Self-driving cars are more similar to humans than we could ever imagine.

A learning network is embedded in a vehicle equipped with lasers, radar, cameras, GPS, and actuators that bring environmental information into the network.[7] Programmers give it a goal to navigate the environment safely, a way to measure its success against it, and a few constraints to point it in the right direction. Then they turn the car on, training it through experience, with each move tuning the network until it learns to drive.

The vehicle doesn't know much when turned on for the first time.[8] The programmer hardcodes a few rules to point it in the right direction, but the rest of the connections form from reaching toward its goal through trial and error.[9] As it bumps into the environment, moves that produce a high or low score carve out the patterns that will eventually enable the car to drive independently. After driving millions of road miles and simulating billions more, the self-driving network makes enough mistakes to teach itself how to drive.[10]

Humans can automate the skill of driving after about 50 hours of experience.[11] Driverless cars learn with a network as we do, but it's primitive and takes much longer.[12] Networks in self-driving cars are slow learners that take a crude approach to learning by tuning with almost endless amounts of data until they establish the patterns to drive. Of course, not every driverless car on the road is trained from the bottom up. Programmers take a base model, train the network from scratch, then clone and deploy it across an entire fleet of vehicles.[13]

Fully autonomous self-driving cars are not commercially available, and it will still be some time before that becomes a reality. Until then, cars as we know them will gradually become more automated, eventually evolving to drive independently without human assistance. Before becoming fully autonomous, we will share driving responsibilities with the car, as we work together to navigate the roadways successfully.

As self-driving capabilities increase, human drivers' responsibilities will decrease until we are no longer required to assist. In 2014, the Society of Automotive Engineers (SAE) developed a classification of levels outlining the progression of self-driving automation in vehicles, ranging from zero to full automation.[14]

Self-Driving Levels

- **Level 0 - No Automation:** The traditional vehicle where we do all the driving.
- **Level 1 - Driver Assistance:** The vehicle has one or two automatic functions, such as adaptive cruise control or lane-keeping, but we still do the driving.
- **Level 2 - Partial Automation:** The vehicle combines multiple forms of automation to assist with steering, speed control, lane keeping, and maintaining a safe distance. The car can drive on its

own for very short durations, but the driver must remain in control and supervise closely.

- **Level 3 - Conditional Automation:** The car has a brain and can drive autonomously for longer durations under certain conditions, such as on highways, but we must be ready to step in at a moment's notice if it gets stuck.
- **Level 4 - High Automation:** The vehicle handles all driving under normal conditions within a predefined zone, and we can sleep in the back seat if we want. We would only need to step in to help when the car is operating outside its designed footprint or when conditions, such as weather, become too challenging. The car is the primary driver, and we are in a secondary position, acting as the supervisor who intervenes only when the vehicle is stuck or if we just want to drive.
- **Level 5 - Full Automation:** No driver, pedals, or steering wheel are required; the vehicle performs 100 percent of the driving at all times.[15]

Level 3 conditional automation is currently the highest level of self-driving technology commercially available to consumers.[16] This level of automation can drive independently for hours without needing assistance, such as on highways. Still, at any moment, it could encounter a situation where it does not have an adequate response and will tag the human driver in for assistance.[17] When the self-driving system is driving, we continually monitor and take over when it encounters trouble. The car and driver coalesce into a single vehicle, leveraging a pseudo-design in which two separate processing systems work as one unit to navigate the roadway safely.[18]

A self-driving network trains to handle most situations, but there will be times when it encounters something new and may not have an adequate answer. When that happens, the vehicle will disengage and hand control over to the human driver.[19] We take the wheel, acting as a secondary processor that can draw from a lifetime of experience to come up with a solution and bail the self-driving system out.[20]

Disengagements range from minor to severe, serving as lessons the network learns to become an even better driver in the future. Examples include overhanging branches appearing as obstacles, confusion with vehicles in other lanes, and failing to see another car leaving a garage.[21] When these events occur, the human driver takes the wheel to get out of harm's way, returning control to the vehicle once the obstacle is clear.

Once a correction is made, the network can update its model with the solution and use that response the next time it encounters a similar situation. That update may not be in real time, but the general idea is that disengagements continually tune the network's model to improve its overall driving performance. On top of that, the lessons from each vehicle can be shared across the entire fleet, allowing all cars to learn from a single disengagement.[22]

As of 2018, Google's driverless car company, Waymo, had vehicles travelling an average of 11,000 miles between disengagements.[23] Humans, on the other hand, drive hundreds of thousands of miles without incident.[24] Self-driving cars and humans will continue to work together for a while before vehicles that can drive entirely on their own without assistance are commercially available.

CHAPTER 2

The Self-Driving Metaphor

Visualize yourself sometime in the future, sitting in the driver's seat of a new Level 4 high-automation self-driving car. It comes equipped with sensors and a network tuned through experience that automatically adjusts the steering, gas, and brakes to navigate the environment on its own. As the driver, we turn on the car, enter a destination, and it handles the rest.

We sit as the secondary driver in a self-driving first vehicle. Under normal conditions, when traveling to a destination, the car makes the decisions, while we watch it drive. We are the supervisor at the wheel, overseeing a self-driving system. As the secondary driver, we serve as an additional level of processing that can take over when the car encounters an error or when we simply want to take control. Both the car and the driver work together to successfully navigate the environment.

By default, the vehicle is the primary driver, providing instant responses to everything it encounters. As the secondary driver, we experience the car's automatic decisions and can take the wheel afterward, but we have no say in its initial response. Let's assume the car accelerates while driving. As the driver, we feel the result of that decision and assess whether it is moving too fast. Only after appraising the car's automatic acceleration can we take control and apply the brakes.

As the secondary driver of an automatic system, we can take over whenever we want or when the vehicle needs us to. Naturally, we take a passive role because the car can drive independently, and there is no reason to intervene in situations it can handle. In general, the vehicle performs around 80-95 percent of the driving, and we take the wheel for the remaining percentage when it gets stuck.

Humans have been using metaphors to explain what it means to be a living person with a brain since the beginning of our existence.[25] One of the oldest, dating back to the time of the Buddha, is that we are the rider on an elephant.[26]

In *The Happiness Hypothesis*, author Jonathan Haidt explains that each of us is a rational rider positioned on top of an emotional elephant.[27] We hold the reins and make decisions, but the elephant can get hungry or scared at any time, overpowering the rider to do what it wants. The elephant provides instant reactions, impulses, and desires, while the thoughtful rider directs it.[28] The challenge in life is to use our rational rider to manage our mighty emotional elephant as best we can.

New findings in psychology in the 1990s validated the rider-and-elephant metaphor by showing that the brain has two separate but complementary processing systems. One system is automatic and fast, providing the first response to all we encounter, while the other is slow and deliberate, capable of modulating or overriding the first.[29]

Current discoveries in neuroscience and psychology not only validate the rider-and-elephant metaphor but also surpass it. Advances in AI and self-driving cars offer an opportunity to further evolve the metaphor, deepening our understanding of what it means to be human. The modern version of the rider-and-elephant is that we are the driver inside a Level 4 high-automation self-driving human vehicle.

Our brain comprises many interconnected neural circuits that together function like an automatic self-driving system, processing information and producing instant responses to everything we encounter. On top of that, we have executive circuitry that gives rise to the conscious driver at the wheel who supervises the self-driving system.

Like a Level 4 high-automation car, our human vehicle leverages a pseudo-design to navigate its environment. There is a self-driving system that is always on in the background, serving as the primary driver navigating our environment. We are the driver at the wheel who processes self-driving decisions and decides whether to follow them or take the wheel in corrective action. As the driver, we are a secondary system that can manually override the self-driving vehicle and provide an alternative response.

It is difficult to imagine that we are the secondary driver of an automatic, self-driving vehicle because the illusion of life is that we are the primary driver in complete control. We have been riding in our self-driving human vehicle for so long that we no longer even notice it exists, fully associating with everything it suggests as our own. Research indicates that roughly 80-95 percent of our thoughts and responses are automatic, fitting nicely into the self-driving system, while the rest comes from the driver.[30]

The amount of driving performed by the self-driving system relative to the driver is a spectrum that varies widely from person to person. Some people are asleep at the wheel, allowing the self-driving system to operate unsupervised even though they think they are in control. Others continually engage their driver, closely monitor the self-driving system, and take the wheel in corrective action whenever necessary.

We spend our whole lives unknowingly wiring a self-driving system that, in adulthood, is left unsupervised to drive. Many of its responses are inaccurate, but we align with the driver and rarely challenge them. We will continue to learn about the executive at the wheel and how they can take control of the vehicle with deliberate attention. From there, we explore how anyone can overhaul and rewire their self-driving circuitry through consistent corrective action with their driver.

CHAPTER 3

Conscious and Nonconscious

A Level 4 high-automation car has sensors that collect environmental data, feeding it into a highly trained network that can detect traffic lights, signs, pedestrians, lane markings, vehicles, and weather conditions. With that information, the network can make decisions by selecting the best lane, adjusting speed in traffic, avoiding road hazards, swerving to prevent accidents, or pulling over in an emergency. When driving, the car controls the gas, brake, and steering, automatically adjusting them based on its decisions.

The car manages internal functions, information processing, and automatic responses all on its own. As the driver, we have no visibility into the self-driving system's initial processing and response until they occur. We are the experiencers who process the results of the car's automatic reactions as they arise, deciding whether to accept or take the wheel to correct them.

In the human Level 4 high-automation vehicle, our self-driving system manages over a thousand bodily functions, such as heart rate, digestion, blood filtration, cell generation, and immune function, all to keep the lights on.[31] It has sensors for the eyes, nose, ears, skin, and mouth that collect environmental data, sending it into our network. That information shapes patterns through experience, allowing the self-driving system to automatically respond to everything we encounter.

Our human self-driving vehicle is estimated to process around 11 million bits of information per second, enabling it to sense external objects, process information, and respond instantly.[32] It has reflexive reactions like sneezing, coughing, puking, itching, yawning, and recoiling from pain.[33] Others are emotional and habitual, like when we get angry, laugh, cry, blush, drink coffee, bite our nails, smoke a cigarette, check our phone when it beeps, or smile when others smile at us. Even when we are idle, the vehicle has a default mode that generates mind-wandering and rumination. Our self-driving vehicle always runs in the background, generating the first response to everything we encounter.

The driver equates to consciousness, who is only aware of the result of self-driving decisions as they happen. Everything we are not conscious of is handled by our self-driving system, making those operations nonconscious. For simplicity, the term nonconscious replaces the commonly misunderstood subconscious, which we will define as all functions and processing handled by our self-driving system. Our self-driving system operates in the background nonconsciously, initially outside driver awareness. It is responsible for much of our mental activity and initial responses to all we encounter.[34]

Our self-driving system forms patterns from a lifetime of experience and uses them to respond as it moves through the environment. These are mechanical, emotionless circuits wired through experience that automatically produce emotional and behavioral responses to what we encounter.[35] Our vehicle is the primary driver, selecting from a repository of impersonal responses to navigate the environment.[36] Our nonconscious self-driving system is the first to process information and respond, producing our automatic thoughts, feelings, and actions.[37] Most often, we are the conscious driver who personalizes and makes sense of automatic decisions after they happen.[38]

Our self-driving nonconscious cries during a movie, laughs at someone falling, blushes when embarrassed, accidentally says something rude, ruminates on past or future events, prompts us to watch TV, and constantly checks our phone. We are the conscious driver sitting shotgun at the wheel, constructing an explanation for these self-driving decisions.[39]

As the driver, I become aware of my tears while watching a movie only after the self-driving system triggers them. From there, I can decide whether to cry or suppress my tears. Of course, our driver can also cry on demand, like a seasoned actor, but aside from intentional crying, our tears and other similar emotional reactions initially arise from nonconscious processing.

As the driver, we have no direct access to nonconscious processing until after the self-driving system generates it.[40] The conscious driver provides a second level of processing that accesses a storehouse of memories and knowledge to process the self-driving responses further, coming up with alternatives when needed.[41] The driver is the executive at the wheel, acting as a supervisor who can modify, edit, and override the self-driving system that makes our first decisions.[42]

In the 1970s, after conducting a series of studies, neurophysiologist Benjamin Libet concluded that free will is more like 'free won't, which makes sense because consciousness interacts with self-driving nonconscious decisions after they occur.[43] Studies suggest that the conscious driver processes roughly 16-50 bits per second, compared to the 11 million processed by the nonconscious.[44] The self-driving system does the heavy lifting, while we process the result and only intervene when needed.

When riding inside a Level 4 high-automation car for the first time, we will watch it closely, ready to take the wheel at a moment's notice. After a while, we will trust that the vehicle can navigate successfully on its own, placing our attention elsewhere while it drives. We can look at our phone, call someone, meditate, or go to sleep, leaving the vehicle unattended while it navigates with minimal supervision.

If the car suddenly brakes, swerves, or signals for assistance, we'll snap to attention and take over, using our driver's additional processing power to get out of the situation. We can also take control whenever we want, if we're bored and want to drive instead. The balance between how much the human drives and how much the vehicle drives will vary from person to person. Some people may only take the wheel when necessary, while others may still enjoy driving from time to time. On average, the Level 4 high-automation car can perform up to 95 percent of the driving, while we engage intermittently to help when it gets stuck.

Our human vehicle uses a similar setup: the nonconscious self-driving system drives most of the time, and the conscious driver only intervenes when an error occurs. Think of when we encounter a broken escalator. The self-driving system thinks the escalator is moving, but the driver steps in to confirm it isn't and takes manual control to help us walk up. Although we believe we are in control, our driver typically only takes the wheel when an error occurs. Generally, our driver becomes so accustomed to our self-driving system that they leave it to drive unsupervised, as we rarely second-guess its automatic responses.

We think we are the primary driver, but experts suggest that our nonconscious self-driving system produces between 80-90 percent of our thoughts and actions.[45] Stem cell DNA scientist Bruce Lipton even suggests that up to 95 percent of our daily responses may be nonconscious.[46] Our self-driving system is always driving unless we take the wheel from it. How much overall driving our self-driving system performs is a spectrum that varies for each of us, depending on how often we engage our conscious driver.

If we are continually disengaged, sleeping at the wheel, never intervening with the self-driving system, then it could drive up to 95 percent of the time. On the other hand, if we use our conscious driver to closely supervise the self-driving system and frequently take the wheel to correct it, we could lower that to 80 percent. Either way, we are behind the wheel of a self-driving system that routinely handles most of the driving.

Some of the responses from the human vehicle are inaccurate, but because the driver agrees with them, they go unchallenged and remain unchanged. We can all benefit from waking our driver to challenge our self-driving responses more often. Every time the driver overrides the self-driving system with a new response, it creates a new pattern that can eventually replace the initial automatic one. As we progress, we will continue to build awareness around how nonconscious we really are and learn to actively use our driver to rewire our self-driving system for success and better health.

CHAPTER 4

System 1 and System 2

When riding in a Level 4 high-automation car, two systems work together to navigate the environment successfully. The first is the automatic self-driving system, which makes the initial decision, while the second is the driver, who can take manual control of the car when required. Similarly, recent discoveries in neuroscience and psychology now reveal that the human brain uses two complementary processing systems to navigate its environment.

In 1977, William Schneider and Richard Shiffrin introduced the idea that the brain uses two distinct but parallel systems to process information: one that is automatic and the other controlled.[47] These have since evolved into System 1 and System 2, going mainstream in 2011 with the book *Thinking, Fast and Slow* by psychologist Daniel Kahneman.[48] Collectively, these two systems are responsible for cognition, emotion, and behavior, accounting for every decision we make.[49] System 1 fits into the human Level 4 high-automation vehicle as the self-driving system, while System 2 makes up our conscious driver.[50]

System 1 is always on; fast, automatic, and continually generating suggestions.[51] Anytime we open our eyes, it generates a three-dimensional projection that visually represents objects in our line of sight, their orientation in space, and labels what they are.[52] With that, System 1 has an interface that allows it to sense and respond to its environment.

Think of a self-driving car that responds to everything it comes across. If a pedestrian jumps in front of the vehicle, it will stop; if another car swerves into its lane, it will move to avoid a collision. The car senses its environment, processes information, and automatically responds, with the driver experiencing the result.

Our human vehicle operates similarly, with System 1 working in the background to process information and instantly react to what it encounters.[53] These are automatic survival, habitual, and intuitive responses that are hardwired or tuned through experience, operating nonconsciously, initially outside of conscious driver awareness.[54]

Every automatic decision a Level 4 high-automation car makes will have a corresponding vehicular response. Likewise, in humans, most rapid System 1 responses activate corresponding neurochemicals, leading to physiological changes our driver experiences and labels as emotions.

Nonconscious System 1 is fast-acting and automatic, using learned associations backed by chemicals to generate emotional responses to what it encounters.[55] These are impersonal reactions that are sensitive to context, forming our biases and preconceived notions, which fire automatically, resulting in our emotional responses.[56] Most of the feelings and emotions we experience originate from System 1 circuits, initially outside conscious awareness.

When we are idle, and there is minimal external input, the brain's default mode network activates, engaging in spontaneous System 1 processing that we experience as mind-wandering.[57] These are also self-driving thoughts, backed by chemicals, that the driver experiences as they happen.

All the nonconscious thoughts and actions that originate in the self-driving System 1 come from its circuits located beneath the brain's outer surface. These are medial regions, located deeper in the brain toward the middle, wrapping around a core of subcortical parts that together form the self-driving circuits that drive us.[58]

Nonconscious Self-Driving System 1 Responses

- Looking at someone attractive.
- Honking at someone who cuts us off.
- Checking our phone when it beeps.
- Drinking coffee when we wake up.
- Punching something out of frustration.
- Recognizing a friend in a crowd.
- Instantly knowing the answer to 2+2.
- Ruminating on a conflict with someone.
- Daydreaming about winning the lottery.
- Excitement when our favorite sports team wins.

As we can see, nonconscious System 1 works hard, accounting for an estimated 80% of our thoughts, actions, and behaviors, while we are the driver experiencing it all.[59] Who we think we are and identify with as "I" is System 2, our conscious driver.[60] Lateral circuitry, roughly residing along the brain's outermost surface, represents our executive capacities to plan, reason, and exercise self-control, which gives rise to our System 2 driver.[61]

System 2 is slow and deliberate, serving as an additional level of processing that involves conscious reasoning.[62] The automatic operations of System 1 generate surprisingly complex patterns of ideas, but only slower System 2 can construct thoughts in an orderly series of steps.[63] System 2 is the driver at the wheel, with additional processing power to evaluate System 1 decisions and take control of the vehicle when required.

When System 1 encounters a situation it does not have an answer for, it grabs the attention of our conscious System 2 driver for help.[64] When engaged, System 2 provides an additional level of processing that the driver uses to step in with an original solution, allowing us to rise above our purely automatic System 1 responses. When someone insults us, and we want to snap back or send an angry email, that is System 1. Catching that response and not responding is the heroic effort of our System 2 driver.[65]

Our conscious System 2 driver can take the wheel to control and override System 1 responses with corrective action at any time. Although we can use System 2's extra processing power to intervene with our self-driving responses when needed, we rarely do. In most cases, System 2 is generally in a low-effort mode, disengaged as we sleep at the wheel, while System 1 drives unchallenged.

Our System 2 circuitry is largely underdeveloped at birth, leaving System 1 unvetted to process our early experiences as it lays the foundation for the automatic responses that drive us. Our System 2 driver develops from childhood through our mid-twenties, taking on a more active role in vetting System 1 responses. As we grow into adulthood, System 1 generates impressions, intuitions, intentions, and feelings for everything we encounter. If our System 2 driver endorses them, they can become our System 1 beliefs and voluntary actions.[66]

By early adolescence, our System 2 driver has helped shape the automatic self-driving System 1 that will guide much of our lives. Since we helped to wire our self-driving responses, we are aligned with them and rarely interject. System 1 says, “I am not good enough,” “I can’t do that,” “I am not talented,” “I am stupid,” “I can’t change,” “I can’t be successful,” and System 2 agrees, letting them go unchecked. System 2 can take the wheel from the self-driving system whenever it wants, but it rarely does because it usually agrees with System 1's suggestions.[67]

Our conscious System 2 driver oversees self-driving System 1, agreeing or disagreeing with its decisions. When we agree with a self-driving decision, we reinforce and lock it in as the appropriate automatic response for next time. If the driver disagrees and overrides the self-driving system with an alternative thought or action, that response can become the new automatic System 1 response next time.

When we override a self-driving decision with our driver, that new System 2 response replaces the automatic one. By repetitively correcting self-driving responses with our driver, we can overhaul and rewire System 1. In that way, anyone can use our System 2 driver more often to retrain System 1 to drive better. If we don't challenge System 1 responses, we'll only reinforce them, and they will remain the same. However, if we strategically use our conscious driver to take corrective action over self-driving System 1 responses that do not serve us, we can rewire it to drive us with greater balance. It has taken a lifetime to wire our brains the way they are, and it may take a lifetime to rewire them using our System 2 driver. Just engaging the driver to realize how automatic we are is a step in the right direction.

CHAPTER 5

Goals and Measuring Success

AI programmers who design a self-driving car start by building an artificial neural network, setting a goal for it to navigate its environment safely, and providing a way to measure success against that goal.[68] From there, they turn the vehicle on, and it collects data from its sensors. As it interacts with its environment, the network forms functional patterns based on moves that maximize its score, until it can drive itself. All an artificial network needs is a goal and feedback data; everything else is learned through trial and error.[69] The network may come prewired with some base patterns that provide constraints as a starting point, but its specific wiring is shaped by experience.

If we view nature as an AI company building living-robot products with biological networks, Homo sapiens would be its mass-produced line of products with awareness, leveraging a design similar to that of a Level 4 high-automation vehicle. Each of us has a neural network equipped with the goals of survival and procreation, the motivation to reach them, and a way to measure success against those targets.[70] Evolution prewires some patterns of hard-earned lessons from the past that help us achieve our inborn goals, while the rest of the network flexibly wires through experience as we navigate our environment.

A Level 4 high-automation car comes with an internal point system that awards high scores for actions that support its goal of safe navigation. Staying in the lane, maintaining a safe following distance, and smoothly adjusting the gas and brakes are maneuvers that receive high scores. Driving outside the lane, slamming the brakes, or misidentifying objects earns a low score. The point system provides feedback that guides how the network connects toward its goal.

In humans, feelings are like our internal point system that nature installs to guide us as we wire our network toward survival and procreation.[71] Generally, acts that promote these goals produce feelings of pleasure, while those that don't cause pain.[72] Activities such as drinking coffee, having sex, and acts of kindness get a high pleasure score, whereas touching a hot stove, rejection, or shame get a high pain score.

Feelings are momentary responses to what we encounter that inform us about what to pursue or avoid.[73] They're meant to be temporary, so we can learn the lesson and move on. Making feelings fleeting ensures we repeat what pleases us to feel the rush again. Likewise, if something causes pain, we wouldn't want to feel its sting forever, so it fades, and we learn to avoid it.[74] Feelings act like the point system that tells us what is beneficial or harmful as it relates to survival and procreation.[75]

Nature doesn't want us to be happy; it wants us to live long enough to reproduce, and feelings are the gauge of success toward that end.[76] Our self-driving system automatically assigns a pain or pleasure score to everything we encounter, while we, as the driver, experience, evaluate, and personalize the result. A lifetime of the driver appraising feelings generated by the self-driving system gradually wires our brain with what we approach and avoid according to our inborn goals.[77]

In addition to goals and a way to measure success, AI programmers hardwire artificial networks with general rules as constraints that help it wire toward its target. The Level 4 high-automation car is programmed to prioritize human safety, stay in its lane, and avoid obstacles. These are foundational rules that complement its primary goal of navigating the roadway safely, providing the training wheels the network uses to learn to drive independently. Programmers establish behavioral parameters that the car expresses through driving until it tunes a network that achieves its goal. The rules provide a framework shaped by experience that determines exactly how the network wires.

Nature takes a similar approach, installing built-in behavioral templates that we embellish through experience.[78] We are born with the goals of survival and procreation, along with hardwired behavioral tendencies that set the bounds for how our brain wires.[79] We are not born a blank slate; nature installs proven lessons from the past that point us in the right direction.[80]

These are not rigid programs, but flexible templates that govern defense, social interactions, decision-making, and reproduction, which we refine through experience.[81] For example, with our defense template, we are born with fears of falling and loud noises, but fears of airplanes, police, hospitals, or public speaking develop through experience. It is beneficial to come hardwired with basic worries, but we also need the flexibility to learn new ones unique to our environment and personal experience.

Caring what others think, wanting to outdo rivals, seeking high social rank, and defending what's ours are innate drives that push us toward our goals.[82] If we can get to the top of the pecking order, our odds of finding a mate increase. So do our chances of producing offspring.[83] Although our network comes preinstalled with behavioral templates, it is our unique experiences that determine their expression.

Our genes only care about being passed down to the next generation, so they equip our self-driving system with goals, feelings, and rules to make that happen.[84] At the same time, we are the driver overseeing the self-driving system, who can decide whether or not to follow its decisions. For some, the driver is asleep at the wheel, rarely intervening as the vehicle drives with minimal supervision. While others may be awake, closely supervising the self-driving system and taking corrective action more often.

Although self-driving goals, feelings, and templates guide us toward survival and procreation, we all have a conscious driver inside that can rise above it all. Our self-driving System 1 provides the initial response, but our System 2 driver has the ultimate say. If we use our executive circuitry to its fullest potential, we can override System 1's self-driving impulses and wire our brains the way we want.

Our genes may have an agenda, pushing us in a specific direction, but it is our conscious driver who can ultimately decide where we go. Each of us can wake up our driver within to challenge our self-driving system and take the wheel to direct how our brain wires. Deliberately engaging our driver is our hidden power for wiring our network toward the life we want. By directing our experience, we can direct how our network wires.

CHAPTER 6

Input and Output

Artificial neural networks are powerful processors, but they are nothing without inputs to collect data and outputs to respond. A Level 4 high-automation car has many input sensors that collect environmental data and send it into the network for processing. From there, the network has output connections throughout the vehicle, enabling it to control all internal functions and drive.

The network's output connections enable it to automatically respond by adjusting the gas, brake, and steering based on what it processes. If the network detects an obstacle and determines it needs to brake, the output components instantly comply. The network performs the processing, while the inputs and outputs are strictly mechanical mechanisms that bring in data and allow it to act.

Our brain has mechanical inputs and outputs much like an artificial network in a Level 4 high-automation car. In the human body, both inputs and outputs are managed by the peripheral nervous system, which is connected to the central nervous system, which consists of the brain and spinal cord.

The input includes our eyes, ears, nose, mouth, and skin sensors that bring environmental information into our neural network for processing.[85] The output has two main branches: one connects to glands and organs to regulate internal functions, and the other connects to muscles that enable physical movement in response to what we encounter.

The network in a Level 4 high-automation car has complete control over all the vehicle's internal functions while driving. When in park, it regulates the engine at an idle resting state, working just hard enough to keep the car running. When in drive, the network applies the gas, increasing engine speed to accelerate the vehicle. Once at the desired speed, it automatically adjusts the gas and brake as required to maintain it. When the car needs to stop, the network triggers the brake, and the engine slows back to its resting state.

The artificial network serves as the primary self-driving system that controls the car and automatically responds to its environment. As the driver, we are a secondary system that experiences the result of the network's decisions. We only influence the gas and brake when we are actively driving; the rest of the time, the self-driving system controls them.

Within the human vehicle, the brain uses the autonomic nervous system, which is connected to internal glands and organs, to regulate their activity.[86] These output connections allow our self-driving system to control functions such as breathing, heart rate, digestion, and salivation.[87] The autonomic system has two general channels: the sympathetic, which excites, and the parasympathetic, which inhibits.[88] These are the human vehicle's equivalent of a car's gas and brake that our self-driving system automatically adjusts to drive us.[89]

Similar to a high-automation car, when we are at rest, our self-driving system maintains our heart rate and breathing at a baseline setpoint to keep us alive. When we engage in physical activity or encounter a threat, our vehicle's speed increases. In response, our self-driving system triggers the sympathetic nervous system, like a car's accelerator, raising our heart and respiratory rates to meet the required demand. It will continue to use the autonomic systems, sympathetic gas, and parasympathetic brake to maintain that speed as needed for the duration of that activity. When we stop moving, or the threat passes, the parasympathetic brake activates, bringing us back to our original baseline resting state.

All day long, our self-driving system continually adjusts our autonomic gas and brakes to rise to the occasion and return to our ideal setpoint, in a process called homeostasis. Homeostasis is the process by which the body maintains internal parameters, such as temperature, heart rate, and pH, at specific set points to support optimal performance.[90]

Our thoughts, actions, and environment continually influence our gas or brakes, shifting us from our ideal set point. Homeostasis brings us back to baseline, restoring balance. If we go for a run, our sympathetic nervous system will increase our heart rate and metabolism, raising our overall body temperature. When we're done, homeostasis automatically kicks in, activating the parasympathetic brake to restore our stable core temperature.[91] Our internal organs fluctuate throughout the day to meet the demands of internal and external influences, with homeostasis keeping them all in balance.[92]

The nonconscious self-driving system uses the autonomic output to regulate our internal functions. Operating outside conscious control, it uses our sympathetic accelerator and parasympathetic brake to automatically respond to our environment, returning to our ideal setpoints when the event passes.[93] Our self-driving system accelerates and brakes all day long, initially outside our awareness, influencing our heart rate like an engine. As the driver, we cannot directly control our heart rate; our self-driving system determines its speed.[94]

Even though the self-driving system manages our heart rate, our driver can indirectly influence its speed by intentionally slowing our breath. When we exhale slowly, it slows the heart and triggers the parasympathetic brake, helping to restore balance. By consciously attending to our breath, our driver can take the wheel from the self-driving system and manually apply the brakes whenever our vehicle accelerates. Slowing our breath with the driver is how we can mimic homeostasis, bringing ourselves into balance whenever we want.

Later chapters will explore how a lifetime of experience can miscalibrate the brain, making the self-driving system prone to triggering chronic acceleration all outside our awareness. When our vehicle accelerates too often, homeostasis struggles to maintain balance, and our vehicle begins to break down. Since our self-driving system does the driving, we feel helpless as it drives recklessly, while we do our best to hang on. Fortunately, consciously slowing our breath is our secret power for taking control of our vehicle and applying the brake whenever we need to.

CHAPTER 7

Brain Basics

Each of us is a human vehicle equipped with a three-pound neural network of the same general design, which consumes 20 percent of our energy just to keep running.[95] Our brain is a mass of densely interconnected structures and regions that form several circuits that together make up our self-driving and driver functions. Before looking into each of these circuits, it is essential to understand the individual regions and structures that contribute to them.

Picture the brain as a core of inner structures covered by an outer surface called the cortex.[96] There is a thin layer of cortex called the allocortex that directly surrounds structures near the center of the brain. Covering that is another thick, six-layered sheet of cells called the neocortex, forming the brain's outer shell.[97] Our driver circuits lie on the outermost lateral surface of the neocortex. In contrast, self-driving circuits involve everything beneath it, including the medial neocortex, much of the allocortex, and all the structures they surround toward the brain's center.[98]

The cortex surrounds the inner core of structures forming the foundation of our automatic self-driving circuits. To work well, a Level 4 high-automation network must be able to take in data and integrate it throughout. For that, we have the thalamus at the center of the brain, acting as a convergence zone that takes in and relays all incoming sensory information, except smell, to relevant circuits throughout the brain.[99]

As data flows through the network, a point system is needed to gauge whether an action helps achieve the goal. In humans, this system is feelings, and they inform us about what to approach or avoid in the name of survival and procreation as we interact with the world. Positioned below the thalamus is the hypothalamus, which produces hormones that regulate internal feelings relating to arousal, hunger, and fatigue. As drivers, we experience the results, labeling them as emotions that move us toward or away from our inborn goals.[100] The thalamus integrates information, while the hypothalamus generates immediate feelings, informing us what is beneficial or harmful, as we shape our brain through experience.

Next, the network in a Level 4 high-automation car must be able to remember its experiences and recall them instantly to navigate its environment successfully. Our brain uses the hippocampus, a seahorse-shaped structure that encodes experience as memories, distributes them across the brain, and retrieves them as needed.[101]

Additionally, a self-driving car must be able to learn new functions that can be stored and executed automatically at any time. Our brain has the basal ganglia, which serve as an autopilot system that automates what we do the most, executing them at a moment's notice. These become our habits, behaviors, and skills, learned through experience, that are used without requiring driver input.[102]

Lastly, a self-driving car needs a way to scan its environment and respond instantly to what it encounters. Our amygdala performs that function, acting as a self-driving scanner that is constantly on the lookout for cues in the environment related to defense or pleasure. If something relevant is detected, it will trigger an automatic full-body emotional response.[103] Instantly ducking from a foul ball heading our way while sitting safely behind protective mesh at a baseball game is an example of the amygdala orchestrating a whole-body response outside conscious awareness to save our lives.

The neocortex, which forms the thick outer shell surrounding the structures at the center of the brain, divides into the left and right hemispheres. Although divided, they connect via the corpus callosum, a large bundle of nerve fibers that carries signals between them. It integrates information and connects the two hemispheres, allowing them to function as a single collective network.[104]

Each hemisphere divides into four regions, or lobes: occipital, temporal, parietal, and frontal. The occipital lobe, positioned at the back of the brain, is associated with vision.[105] The temporal lobes are on the sides, near the temples, and are involved in hearing and memory. The parietal lobe, located at the top of the brain, supports spatial awareness and sensory processing.[106] The frontal lobe is at the front of our head, accounting for one-third of the brain's mass.[107] The back of the frontal lobe helps control motor function. At the same time, the frontmost portion is the prefrontal cortex, which is subdivided into many regions and is associated with social behavior, language, reasoning, and executive function.[108]

All mammals have a prefrontal cortex, but the lateral regions are more developed in primates and are most complex in humans.[109] It is a central hub for processing, sending, and receiving signals from both the medial self-driving and lateral driver circuits that connect to it.[110] Our self-driving circuits connect to the medial sections and are involved in survival, intuitive reactions, and mind-wandering.[111] Whereas our driver circuits, responsible for reasoning, planning, and self-control, connect to the outer lateral sections.[112]

Although this chapter has described the roles of individual structures, it's necessary to understand that no part of the brain acts in isolation. Every process in the brain arises from circuits involving multiple interconnected regions.[113] Our brain is not a collection of isolated centers that contribute to a clear-cut process or function on their own.[114] It is a highly parallel integrated network functioning as a single unit that sends signals through complex circuits that together give rise to who we are.[115]

Any part of the brain can be part of many circuits and contribute to many functions.[116] As a result, multiple hemispheres, regions, or structures can be involved in any single task. In the following chapters, we will use the regions and structures discussed in this chapter as a foundation for explaining the specific circuits that make up our self-driving and driver systems.

CHAPTER 8

Self-Driving Survival Circuits

When driving, a Level 4 high-automation car uses radar and cameras to scan for objects, pedestrians, vehicles, and safety-related signs. It will automatically respond as soon as danger is detected, adjusting the gas, brake, and steering to get out of harm's way. If another vehicle is hurtling toward it, the high-automation car will instantly detect it and slam on the accelerator to avoid a collision. In another scenario, the car may brake to avoid colliding with a bicycle that crosses its path. These are rapid responses relating to emergencies that the self-driving car deploys, designed to keep us alive. As the person in the driver's seat, we experience the results of the self-driving system's acceleration and braking. We are in a secondary position, with no involvement in the vehicle's initial decisions until they occur.

The human vehicle operates the same way, using self-driving circuits to scan its environment and respond automatically, without driver input. We are the conscious driver in the seat, but not initially in control, as our self-driving system is the primary driver, providing an instant response to everything we encounter. Our most fundamental self-driving circuits relate to defense, food, and sex. These are survival circuits meant to achieve our inborn goal of staying alive and reproducing.[117] They continuously operate in the background, nonconsciously steering our behavior before driver awareness.[118]

For defense, think of our heart racing when pulled over by the police. For food, remember a time when chasing an ice cream truck after hearing its music. For sex, consider the butterflies we experience when texting someone we like, or our eyes automatically moving toward someone attractive. Each of these responses originates from the self-driving system, and we are the driver who experiences the outcome. We have nothing to do with the initial detection or response; our job as the driver is to decide whether to go with it or not. Any sight, sound, scent, sensation, or taste in our environment can instantly trigger our survival circuits, while we, as the conscious driver, interpret the result.

Our amygdala, hippocampus, and hypothalamus are essential structures near the center of the brain that contribute to our survival circuits.[119] From birth onward, the amygdala associates experiences with specific defense, food, and sex circuits, using the hippocampus to encode them as memories tied to people, places, and time that are distributed across the brain for long-term storage.[120]

From there, our amygdala scans the environment 12 to 100 times per second, searching for any stored memories tied to survival.[121] If it finds a match, it automatically activates the corresponding defense, food, or sex circuit associated with that memory, triggering the hypothalamus to deliver a supporting full-body acceleration or brake response.[122]

Some survival-related cues come hardwired at birth, while others take shape through personal experience. Our entire lives, the amygdala stamps experiences relating to food, sex, and defense onto survival circuits, orchestrating an immediate automatic response the moment it detects them.[123]

The wiring for survival circuits is simple: information from outside flows into the amygdala, and it uses output connections to control corresponding internal responses.[124] The output produces nonconscious physiological adjustments, like heart rate, tension, and hormonal shifts, that we later interpret as emotions.[125]

We are the drivers experiencing and piecing together the results of self-driving survival circuits, labeling them as emotional states.[126] The amygdala automatically fires defense, food, and sex circuits, triggering physiological responses that we later appraise as fear, anxiety, frustration, hunger, and lust. Emotional feelings are the driver's interpretation of whole-body responses organized by the amygdala.[127]

The amygdala cares only about survival and procreation; if we are not alive, we cannot reproduce, so it places a premium on defense.[128] Researchers estimate that roughly two-thirds of the cells in the amygdala are dedicated to threat detection and response.[129] As soon as it detects a cue linked to danger, it activates the corresponding defense circuit, producing an equivalent physiological and motor response.[130] These are hardwired, self-driving fight-or-flight reactions, built in by nature, that the amygdala links to threatening experiences. Defense reactions are essentially the same across all humans, but what triggers them is unique to each person's history.[131] As the driver, we label the outcome of amygdala-driven defensive survival responses as emotions like fear and anxiety.[132]

Although no single brain structure works alone, multiple areas are involved in processing fear, and the amygdala is essential for coordinating rapid defensive responses.[133] All circuits that pass through the amygdala, including those responsible for defense, follow a similar design: each has an input and an output that together drive automatic behavior.[134]

Neuroscientist Joseph LeDoux discovered that sensory information reaching the amygdala travels along two paths that he calls the low road and the high road. These roads have been extensively studied in defense responses, and they will become the primary focus as we attempt to understand how self-driving the amygdala and our survival circuits really are.

The low road is a direct route from the thalamus to the amygdala, giving it immediate access to raw sensory input before the cortex processes it.[135] This shortcut allows the amygdala to quickly scan for threat cues and trigger instant responses to save our lives, before we know what's happening.

The low road is short and fast, meant for speed rather than accuracy, when facing potential danger.[136] This path provides the amygdala with raw sensory data about a stimulus, like its relative size, speed, or intensity.[137] It's a rough, rapid first-level self-driving response that occurs before higher brain regions can process what's happening. These low-road responses are known as amygdala hijacks, which describe moments when the brain's threat detection system responds before we consciously recognize a threat.[138]

A great example of an amygdala hijack is the viral Snapchat filter displaying a spider on the face of anyone it points at. Unsuspecting friends and family look into it, see a tarantula on their face, and immediately slap it off in panic as though it's real. Although the spider is fake, it's real to the amygdala. The raw input triggers a full-body behavioral and physiological fight-or-flight response before conscious awareness even has a chance to evaluate the situation and interject.[139]

The hallmark of an amygdala hijack is the immediate overreaction followed by the realization: "I overreacted… what just happened?"[140] These moments are nothing to be embarrassed about, because they are low-road amygdala responses designed to act first and ask questions later, all in the name of survival, to keep us alive.

Other examples of hijacks are the rage we experience when a car cuts us off, flinching when someone scares us, or pulling our hand away when we touch a hot object. Each one is an emotionally charged, instant reaction linked to defense.

Although amygdala hijackings are most commonly studied in the context of defense and fear, research also shows they are present in responses to pleasure and reward.[141] Addictive patterns, like reaching for a snack when feeling bored, lighting a cigarette in a moment of anxiety, or pouring a drink after a stressful call, can also be fast-acting nonconscious hijack reactions triggered by the amygdala.[142]

Information traveling along the second path passes through the cortex for further processing before reaching the amygdala, providing it with more refined details about the object or experience.[143] This slower route serves as a second level of amygdala processing, delivering additional information about a stimulus so the amygdala can make more accurate decisions.[144] The low road takes roughly twelve milliseconds to come up with a response, whereas the high road takes twice as long.[145] The high road provides the amygdala with more context when time is not a factor, or to double-check the accuracy of low-road responses.

In the spider filter example, the low road initiates the panic slap, while milliseconds later, the high road provides more context, telling the amygdala it's not a real spider. At that point, the amygdala can correct its initial decision by providing another response. The low road sacrifices accuracy for speed, while the high road offers increased precision at the cost of time.

Both roads are medial circuits, part of our nonconscious self-driving system.[146] They bring information into the amygdala for processing, where it makes a decision and triggers an equivalent output response. The amygdala is a nonconscious information processor, regardless of the path from which it receives information.[147] The low and high roads provide two levels of information for the self-driving amygdala to use in decision-making.

After the amygdala processes input information, it uses output connections to the hypothalamus and other brainstem structures to produce chemicals appropriate to the activated survival circuit. The sympathetic and parasympathetic channels of the hypothalamus allow the amygdala to accelerate and brake our body, like a car, in response to what we encounter. Each type of survival circuit has a corresponding gas or brake response, enabling the body to automatically adjust to what it encounters.

Our fight-or-flight response is tied directly to acceleration.[148] When the amygdala detects a threat, it triggers our sympathetic gas response, releasing adrenaline to increase heart rate, blood pressure, respiration, and muscle tension.[149] Blood is diverted from the organs to the limbs, temporarily shutting down non-essential functions such as digestion, reproduction, and relaxation, to support the required motor response.[150] Once the body is fully accelerated, cortisol is released to sustain the heightened state for the duration of the threat, whether for a few minutes or hours.[151] When the danger passes, homeostasis activates the parasympathetic brake to return the body to its resting baseline.[152]

The human vehicle continuously accelerates to rise to the occasion and returns to its resting idle state when the moment passes. Occasional bursts of speed to meet the demand of a threat are expected and a regular part of our design. But if we continually accelerate in response to persistent arguments, deadlines, exams, or bad bosses, it puts added stress on our vehicle, eventually taking a toll.[153] When acceleration is chronically triggered all day long, the stress adds up, causing continual wear and tear, which is difficult for the body to sustain over long periods.[154]

Every human vehicle has an overall stress load limit that it can handle before it begins to degrade. Infrequent threats trigger acceleration, with homeostasis activating the brake to bring us back into balance and cool our engine. If the defensive acceleration response is triggered too often, homeostasis can't keep up and struggles to maintain balance. Over time, we run hot and start to break down, leading to mental and physical decline.[155]

Chronic fight-or-flight responses put too much stress on our bodies, leading to cognitive impairment, cardiovascular disease, diabetes, and compromised immune function. They also have links to depression, anxiety, burnout, and post-traumatic stress disorders.[156]

Chronic stress is challenging because the amygdala triggers our automatic survival responses outside driver awareness. Research estimates that the amygdala scans the environment roughly 12-100 times a second, looking for danger in line with our wired experience. It does not matter when in life we first encountered a threat; if it detects a match, it triggers acceleration.[157] Our self-driving system accelerates all day long based on previously imprinted memories, while we, as the driver, interact with the results.

Suppose we are raised in a stable environment. In that case, our amygdala remains well-regulated, firing only during true emergencies before returning to rest.[158] On the other hand, if we grow up in an unstable environment or experience repeated trauma, our defensive circuits will fire often. Over time, repeated activation exercises our amygdala, making it more prone to trigger acceleration. Without realizing it, our experiences can tune and miscalibrate our defensive circuits, making them extra sensitive to threats.[159] When that happens, our self-driving amygdala can become hyperactive, seeing everything as a threat and chronically triggering acceleration without driver participation.

Similar to the rest of the brain, the amygdala is plastic. Studies show that continuous activation makes it grow, much like a muscle responding to exercise.[160] A lifetime of experiences firing our defensive circuits trains our amygdala to be overactive, becoming more sensitive to generating responses related to fear and anxiety.[161] An enlarged amygdala can be associated with PTSD, social phobias, depression, and aggression.[162] Through no fault of our own, life experience can bulk up the amygdala, making it hyper-sensitive to threats, redlining our vehicle outside driver awareness.

When the amygdala chronically triggers acceleration, homeostasis struggles to keep us in balance with the parasympathetic brake. Luckily, we all have lateral circuits that give rise to an executive driver who oversees the self-driving system and can take control when needed.

Our driver experiences the outcomes of self-driving amygdala survival decisions, labeling them as emotional states with the potential to take corrective action. In the spider filter scenario, the amygdala triggered a hijack response before we could consciously act. As the driver, we can only appraise and rationalize the event after the fact, saying something like, "Sorry, that scared me. I thought it was a spider." In other situations where time is not a factor, the driver can engage amygdala processing after making a decision to evaluate whether the response is accurate and determine if corrective action is needed.

The challenge is that our driver generally aligns with our amygdala responses, so we rarely step in to correct them. Think of the nerves we feel from public speaking or the anger that arises when someone cuts us off. We often identify with these amygdala self-driving responses without a second thought. The reality is that the driver can take the wheel after these amygdala reactions and manually apply the brakes whenever they want.[163] Although it is difficult, in many cases, our driver can intervene at any time to activate the parasympathetic brake to restore balance, promote growth, and heal.[164]

By taking the wheel and overriding defensive survival responses after they occur, we can do what homeostasis struggles with and help manually regulate our overactive amygdala. Repeatedly correcting self-driving acceleration by applying the brake over time can shrink and recalibrate the amygdala, making it less sensitive to threats. In later chapters, we will continue to explore our executive circuits and how we can effectively use them to rewire our self-driving system to drive with greater balance.

CHAPTER 9

Self-Driving Intuitive Circuits

When stepping into a Level 4 high-automation car, its network will be wired through experience, fully equipped with an inventory of automatic responses that enable it to drive independently while keeping us safe. When driving, it will intuitively adjust its speed before taking a turn, drive slower in wet weather, avoid known potholes, and yield to public buses re-entering traffic from a stop.

These are learned, general-purpose, automated responses, separate from emergency reactions, that the car uses to drive. They are a repository of general driving behaviors learned through experience that enable the vehicle to respond instantly to environmental sensory information.

The self-driving system is the primary driver that handles all responses while driving. These involve those relating to emergencies and general navigation, which are automatically triggered by what it encounters. The human driver is in a secondary position, experiencing the results of these self-driving decisions, interacting with them as they unfold.

Like a Level 4 high-automation car, the self-driving system for the human vehicle has two general types of automated circuits that respond to cues as we move through our environment. Our survival circuits are one, comprising fast, reactive responses designed to prioritize survival and procreation. The other is our intuitive circuitry that provides a storehouse of learned patterns that guide our everyday behavior.

A lifetime of experience shapes our intuitive circuits, forming the automatic behaviors, beliefs, and attitudes that our self-driving system uses to automatically respond to familiar cues in our environment.[165] These are repeated thoughts and actions that become the habits our human vehicle uses to steer us through life.[166]

Our intuitive circuits function much like those in a Level 4 high-automation car by automatically detecting familiar cues and providing an equivalent response. They enable the human vehicle's self-driving system to seamlessly respond to general situations it has encountered before.

Our intuitive circuitry is a storehouse of learned, involuntary responses, with corresponding states and actions, enabling our self-driving system to respond automatically to cues.[167] Our intuitive circuits check our phone as soon as it beeps, generating excitement, reflexively smile when someone smiles at us, providing a warm feeling, and sigh at the end of a long day, delivering a sense of relief. Each one is an intuitive association linked to emotions and motor movements that our self-driving system automatically executes outside driver awareness.[168] We also experience these with habits like biting our nails, drinking alcohol, or cracking our knuckles, where the response can seem almost impossible to overcome, if we notice it at all.

Our intuitive circuits are nonconscious, self-driving responses to cues unrelated to survival that fire in milliseconds outside our awareness. They shape our first thoughts and actions toward everything we encounter, beyond food, sex, or defense.[169] These general responses automatically trigger corresponding chemicals and motor reactions, all initially outside driver control. We are the conscious driver sitting in a secondary position, interacting with the result of these automatic decisions.

The brain is all about conserving energy, and it does that by automating what we think and do the most.[170] From the second we are born, our intuitive circuits start building an inventory of automatic responses that the self-driving system can use to respond to recurring environmental cues.

The basal ganglia are a central group of brain structures that translate our repeated thoughts and actions into automatic functions, stored and retrieved for instant execution.[171] Brushing our teeth, playing soccer, and holding the door open for someone are part of an inventory of patterns the basal ganglia makes available as automatic functions.[172]

Both medial and lateral circuits connect to the basal ganglia, allowing them to access and trigger stored automated behaviors.[173] The self-driving system uses intuitive circuits to process information and draw from an inventory of automatic functions, using the basal ganglia to respond immediately to what it encounters. That is how the human vehicle automatically scratches an itch, drinks coffee, ties its shoes, and turns its head when someone calls its name, all without driver involvement.[174]

At the same time, our conscious driver can use its connections to the basal ganglia to automatically perform any of the same stored behaviors whenever we take the wheel. We can consciously decide to play soccer or brush our teeth, performing these functions automatically with minimal attention.

Both self-driving and driver circuits have access to the automatic functions stored in the basal ganglia, which they can use when driving. However, experts estimate that our intuitive circuits govern nearly 80 percent of our behaviors.[175] That means our self-driving system is the primary driver selecting from our stored automated patterns as we move through the environment.

When we come into the world, we are like a base model of a Level 4 high-automation car before it's trained through experience. The human network is made of billions of neurons and trillions of connections, equipped with a goal, feelings to measure success against them, and templates to point us in the right direction. It is through experience that we wire specific connections, shaping the network into who we become.

Where attention goes, neural patterns grow.[176] From birth, as we have experiences, our attention focuses on particular aspects of the environment that connect corresponding patterns in the brain. With repetition, the basal ganglia turn what we think and do most often into automatic routines that are available at any time.[177]

Even simple functions like walking, talking, or opening a jar are first learned with attention, and only with repetition do they become automatic.[178] As babies and children, we are sponges that bump into the world, making mistakes, as we form the intuitive circuits that will drive us for the rest of our lives.

Our parents and caretakers are the primary programmers of our self-driving system, wiring the foundation for the automatic behaviors, beliefs, and attitudes that will drive us. They tell us not to swear, to look both ways before crossing the road, that men don't cry, or that mistakes are bad, shaping how we see the world. These protocols are etched into our network as reflexive truths, tuned through repetition rather than through validity. Our brain does not care whether these rules are valid; it impartially wires what we do most, right or wrong.

By the time we are adults, we have unknowingly wired a storehouse of automated responses that our self-driving system uses to drive us, becoming the model for how we see the world. For the most part, we are the driver who agrees with these intuitive responses, never questioning or taking the wheel from the self-driving system.

In reality, our self-driving system's automated model is inaccurate and often steers us in the wrong direction. As we move through our environment, it will say, "We are not good enough," or "we cannot do this or that," producing many false behaviors, beliefs, and attitudes that we see as true. It may also have us continually repeat habits we have automated in response to subtle cues we are not consciously aware of. We live in a perpetual loop, driven by intuitive circuits that do not serve us, but never course-correct because we agree with them.

Our caretakers were our programmers in childhood, but we can be the programmers in adulthood who take control by deliberately using consciousness to rewire our self-driving system in the way we want. When we engage our driver, we begin to realize how automatic we are and expose our false intuitive responses. Taking the wheel from the self-driving system in corrective action overrides its automatic reaction and provides a new option. If we repeat that enough, we can automate another behavior into the basal ganglia, making it available as a new self-driving response.

When I first started listening to audiobooks, I heard new ideas like mistakes are great, genes don't determine who we are, the brain is plastic, and we can change. At first, my intuitive circuits had me scoff in disbelief, telling me they are false. After hearing these statements repeatedly, I began to consciously challenge their validity by applying them to my life, slowly uncovering the truth. Now, these are my new intuitive beliefs, and I scoff when I hear people say contrary thoughts aligned with my old automatic ways of thinking. Just because we have absent-mindedly wired our intuitive circuits does not mean they are correct or that we cannot change them.

The basal ganglia do not ask questions, and our plastic brain will wire whatever we do the most. So, by not following the self-driving system's suggestions and providing an alternative response with our conscious driver, we can automate new behaviors, attitudes, and beliefs. Our executive driver gives each of us the potential to overhaul and rewire our intuitive circuitry in ways that serve us.

The brain does not ask questions; it makes connections, and we are the drivers who can direct its wiring. It doesn't matter how our early experiences wired our perception of the world. We can take the wheel with our driver to rewire the way we want at any time.

CHAPTER 10

Self-Driving Default Mode Circuits

When walking to the park, my self-driving system uses my survival and intuitive circuits to respond to everything I encounter. If, while on the way, a car blows through a stop sign as I cross the street, my amygdala makes me jump out of the way, triggering a scream of rage as it speeds off. Continuing my walk, my intuitive circuits automatically produce thoughts like that person seems "successful," "upset," "crazy," or "friendly" about everyone I see. These are all self-driving responses to cues that automatically occur as we move through the environment.

These responses can capture our driver's attention, prompting us to process them further and decide whether to take corrective action or let them go. We can also deliberately engage attention to take the wheel with our driver and do what we want at any time. I can intentionally stop while walking to the park and mindfully place my attention on a bee pollinating a flower.

Attention is a driver-based function that we will explore in more detail in the next chapter. For now, it's enough to understand that our driver represents another type of circuitry that activates intermittently throughout the day. These are our executive circuits, which are roughly tied to attention, and can be activated by the self-driving system or by the driver.

In the absence of strong cues, our survival and intuitive circuits shift to a less active, low-effort mode, continuing to monitor the environment in a ready state. When those circuits are quiet, the driver does not need to attend to them. At the same time, if our driver is not actively attending to something else, our executive circuits also become less active. Although these circuits are quiet, the brain must always maintain a baseline of mental activity; it never shuts off.[179]

To maintain continuity, the self-driving system keeps a baseline circuit active in the background. Throughout the day, other circuits activate, briefly becoming dominant before fading and defaulting back to the brain's resting state.[180] Known in neuroscience as the default mode network, it functions as a distributed circuit of interconnected brain regions that together produce daydreaming, mind-wandering, and internal storytelling when active.[181]

If we sit on a bench upon arriving at the park and do not engage in anything else, the mind will default to mind-wandering. Whenever we are at rest and not focused on externals, the other circuits quiet, and default mode activity increases, becoming the dominant stream of thought.[182]

The default mode network is present in all human brains, involving populations of neurons distributed across many medial structures and regions, making it a self-driving circuit.[183] When idle and not focused on externals, like in the shower, falling asleep, or walking, our default mode activity generally increases, shifting the mind inward.[184]

When active, the default mode automatically curates a stream of emotionally charged thoughts about past or future scenarios involving ourselves and others.[185] These are ruminations, creative insights, thinking about the future, or reliving the past that are often attributed to mind-wandering or daydreaming.[186]

At rest, the self-driving default mode circuitry can generate heated ruminations replaying a recent fight, excitement while daydreaming about winning the lottery, or empathy when thinking about a struggling friend. Once again, our self-driving medial circuits produce emotionally charged thoughts, and our driver experiences the result.[187]

If a Level 4 high-automation car had a default mode network, it would be like playing the radio anytime it's at rest. When environmental cues are limited, and the driver is disengaged or inattentive, the radio automatically turns on. We have no say in the station; the vehicle would be the DJ, playing whatever it wants whenever it's idle. We are simply the driver experiencing the result. There will be times when we fully engage with it, singing along in enjoyment or begging it to stop if we hate what it's playing. Other times, it will be on in the background, and we won't notice it at all.

Likewise, our human vehicle's self-driving system is like a DJ curating a playlist of wandering thoughts whenever the default mode circuits are active. Each thought that plays has associated emotions, making us feel hopeful, excited, compassionate, anxious, worried, or regretful. As the conscious driver, we have no initial control over when or where the mind wanders; we only have a say after the fact, once we notice it's wandering.[188] Our self-driving system is the DJ that turns on the radio and chooses the song, while we are the driver who can respond to it once it's playing.

For the most part, we do not even notice when our minds wander or when we unknowingly direct our attention to those thoughts. When our driver places attention on our wandering thoughts and gets carried away with them, we fuel them and the accompanying emotions further.

A Harvard study involving over 2,000 adults used an application to ping participants throughout the day, asking them to report what they were doing, how they felt, and where their attention was at that moment.[189] In the end, they found that our minds wander during 47 percent of waking hours, and 30 percent of the time when our attention is actively engaged on a task.[190] From my experience with meditation, our default circuits are much more active, but we can settle on 50 percent as a general rule.

We spend roughly half of our waking hours mind-wandering. During that time, our self-driving system is our DJ, using default mode circuits to automatically curate a stream of thoughts that initially lies beyond our immediate conscious awareness. Additionally, the study found that participants felt less happy when their minds were wandering, regardless of the activity they were engaged in.[191] With this finding, the authors concluded that *a human mind is a wandering mind, and a wandering mind is an unhappy mind*.[192]

When all regions of our default mode circuits are interconnected and functional, they are considered "normal."[193] A normally functioning default mode is well integrated and curates a playlist of more neutral thoughts when active. Nurturance is a necessary factor for the brain to develop as intended.[194] Growing up in a nurturing, supportive environment is associated with healthier, more balanced default mode connectivity. When that happens, our self-driving system tends to produce a more pleasant playlist when the mind wanders.

Exposure to chronic stress has the opposite effect on the brain by weakening neural connections and reducing plasticity. Being raised in a stressful, unstable environment is associated with impaired neural connectivity, leading to altered network development.[195] Upbringing, trauma, anxiety, depression, and even habitual patterns of thought in adulthood can also disrupt brain connectivity.[196] In that case, our default mode circuitry can become miscalibrated, curating a stream of negative thoughts prone to anxiety, resentment, worry, or self-criticism whenever it fires.[197]

Miscalibrated default mode circuits automatically play thoughts of shame as we relive past mistakes, anxiety as we imagine upcoming social events going wrong, regret while reflecting on poor life choices, or worry as we run through fictitious worst-case scenarios. It is as though our default mode is a lousy DJ with an awful playlist, playing distressing songs whenever we are idle. Through no fault of our own, many of us are walking around with miscalibrated default mode circuits that produce harmful content outside our awareness. In reality, a "normal" default mode is more likely a miscalibrated default mode, which explains why a wandering mind is an unhappy mind.

Since default mode circuits are part of the self-driving system, we have no say when they fire, but as the driver, we always have the option to go with or override them with another response. For the most part, we fully associate with our wandering mind, unaware that the stream of thought it generates is the product of a self-driving circuit firing outside our awareness.

When we direct attention to our wandering thoughts and follow them, we strengthen those default mode patterns, making them more likely to generate that content in the future.[198] We fall into a perpetual loop where our default mode curates distressful content that we attach to with our driver, reinforcing and tuning them further, leading to similar thoughts in the future.

If we have a miscalibrated default mode circuit, it isn't broken; it's just poorly tuned. Luckily, the executive driver in all of us has the power to take the wheel from our self-driving system with corrective action and rewire our circuits.

In practice, the default mode is most active when other circuits are quiet. Activating another circuit when the mind wanders is one strategy for interrupting the default mode. More specifically, deliberately engaging driver attention on another object, like our breath, activates our executive circuitry and overpowers the default mode for as long as we can hold our focus.

Intentionally activating our driver with attention lets us take control of the radio and momentarily change the song our default mode DJ is playing. Plasticity dictates that if we repeatedly disrupt the default mode whenever we catch it producing distressing messages, we can weaken those connections and begin to recalibrate those circuits.

Over time, we can rewire and retune our default mode circuits to become more neutral by taking control through attention with our driver. It sounds simple in theory, but it is very difficult in practice, because we usually do not notice when our mind wanders in the first place, or we can't tell the difference. Plasticity works slowly, and recalibrating our default mode does not happen overnight; it is a long process that takes years. Later chapters will fully explain how our driver can use practices in attention, such as mindfulness, to build awareness of our wandering mind as we attempt to rebalance our default mode circuitry.

CHAPTER 11

Executive Driver Circuits

After riding around in a Level 4 high-automation car for long enough, we will eventually become accustomed to its decisions and stop paying attention as it drives with minimal supervision. As the driver, we don't have visibility into the processing that goes into the car's decisions; we only interact with the outcome as it happens.

We are positioned as the secondary driver in a self-driving car that does roughly 80-95 percent of the driving on its own. We are only there to supervise and take the wheel when it gets stuck. If conditions arise that it cannot handle, such as a severe weather event that reduces visibility, the car will pull over, passing control over to us. From there, we can come up with a solution and navigate the situation.

We are the supervisor at the wheel with extra processing power, able to observe what the car is doing and provide alternative responses when required. We can also take the wheel from the self-driving system to drive whenever we like. As the driver, we are passengers who can override the vehicle when needed.

For the most part, we align with the car's decisions, acting as a passive supervisor who only intervenes when necessary. We are in the driver's seat, but our focus is elsewhere, as the vehicle can drive well on its own. As the driver, we can only be aware of what we direct our attention toward; everything else the car does takes place outside our awareness.

The human vehicle employs a design similar to that of a Level 4 high-automation car. Our self-driving system utilizes survival, intuitive, and default mode circuits to drive, while we, the conscious driver, are at the wheel, making sense of what happens.

Our conscious driver is composed of executive circuitry that enables us to monitor, process, and intervene in self-driving decisions, allowing us to take manual control of the vehicle.[199] These executive circuits provide supervisory functions that allow us to monitor, plan, problem-solve, and direct attention.[200]

Signals flow through these executive circuits outside of our awareness, giving rise to our conscious driver, who can take the wheel from the self-driving system to steer our automatic thoughts and actions.[201] These circuits enable executive functions that allow us to process the outcome of lower-level self-driving processing and take control if necessary. The driver isn't aware of the processing that goes into self-driving decisions; they can only piece together the outcome after the fact.[202] Although we are a self-driving first vehicle, our executive circuits save us from being completely autonomous, providing some control over a mainly automatic system.[203]

The lateral surface of our neocortex, which broadly covers the outer surface of our brain, is strongly linked to our executive driver circuitry. The medial neocortex, located beneath it and all the internal structures it surrounds, extending toward the brain's center, comprises our self-driving circuits. Both the driver and self-driving circuits in the brain involve extensive connections spanning multiple regions and structures. They all seamlessly integrate information, giving rise to distinct functions unique to each circuit.

The prefrontal cortex, a region of the brain located behind our forehead, plays a critical role in defining who we are as humans.[204] It has billions of neurons, divided and subdivided into many structural sections, each connected internally and externally to the rest of the brain.[205] Our self-driving survival, intuitive, and default mode circuits converge in the prefrontal cortex's more medial sections, while our driver circuitry connects to its outer lateral sections.[206] With all these connections, the prefrontal cortex acts as a hub of information processing that integrates signals from both our self-driving and driver circuits.[207] It is a central convergence zone that manages signal transfer, sending and receiving information from all circuits to help shape the reality we experience.[208]

The more elaborate the convergence zones present in a species, the more elaborate will be the cognitive capacity of the species.[209] All mammals have a prefrontal cortex, and some, especially primates, have lateral regions, but they are most developed in humans.[210] Our lateral prefrontal cortex divides further into many structures that are themselves made of other substructures, allowing for more convergence than in any other species.[211] Consciousness doesn't reside in the lateral prefrontal cortex, but its neurons, structure, and connections with other regions form circuits that collectively integrate information, playing a critical role in conscious experience.[212]

The convergence of signals within the prefrontal cortex creates a functional workspace where the driver can consciously interact with thoughts and think. The activity from self-driving circuits connecting to the prefrontal cortex flows into the workspace as thoughts. Our driver has a spotlight that can be directed at content within the workspace for additional processing. We can place the spotlight on thoughts arriving from self-driving circuits or deliberately focus it on any topic of our choosing.

The workspace is a playground for thought, and our driver uses the spotlight to take control and think. Whenever the spotlight is on, the driver accesses long-term memory to deliberate and generate solutions.[213] Our driver's ability to process information is limited by what's stored in existing long-term memories.

All the activities taking place in the workspace are referred to as working memory.[214] Some models, such as the Global Workspace Theory, view consciousness as a mental stage where information becomes available for deliberate thought, roughly equating consciousness with working memory.[215] Working memory is our driver's ability to hold information in the workspace while we think, decide, and plan actions.[216] Think of it as a staging area where our driver can shine a spotlight on thoughts for further processing and decide what to do.[217]

When the spotlight is active, our driver can deliberate on what is in focus, using long-term memories distributed throughout the cortex for additional processing.[218] With deliberation, our driver can use long-term memory to devise a list of possible options and choose the best one.[219] Working memory lets our driver direct traffic in our brain, focusing the spotlight on a specific thought, while blocking out competing ones.[220] The convergence in the prefrontal cortex facilitates working memory, but its functions are distributed through circuits spanning widespread regions in the brain.[221]

As the driver, we use working memory for thought and action control.[222] Our executive ability to place the spotlight on our thoughts and behaviors in working memory is called monitoring.[223] Responses from self-driving circuits continually pop into the workspace as thoughts, and we can process them further with our executive circuitry whenever we choose.

The self-driving circuits process information, providing responses that continually feed into the workspace as a steady stream of thoughts. Placing the spotlight on these thoughts gives the driver visibility to them, where they can deliberate further and determine the best decision.[224]

Controlling the spotlight is executive functioning that allows us to monitor our self-driving system, evaluate its actions, and determine whether we should take the wheel to correct its course or let it go unchecked. If the spotlight does not fully shine on a thought in the workspace, it remains untouched by consciousness, never reaching the surface of awareness. The self-driving system is constantly generating thoughts that drift in and out of the workspace, often as nonconscious events that remain unseen by the spotlight.

Unlike our reactive self-driving circuits, our executive circuits are reflective, allowing us to weigh decisions against the goals set by the driver. Activating the spotlight in working memory is how our driver takes the wheel and deliberates on whether a self-driving decision is appropriate. If not, we can generate another option and override its response. At any time, we can use the driver to access working memory, either to appraise self-driving decisions or deliberately use its processing power to think about anything we choose. The challenge is that most of us do not use our spotlight effectively, leaving self-driving responses unchecked as they drift in and out of driver awareness.

Our working memory has two components: a workspace and a spotlight, which acts as a control mechanism that can interact with it.[225] The spotlight is activated by attention, enabling our driver to select content in the workspace and process it further.[226] The information held in our working memory is what we are paying attention to at any given moment.[227]

Attention is an executive function that engages our conscious driver, allowing us to take control of working memory and use it toward our own ends. The attentional spotlight must be on for consciousness to occur, but we are not conscious every time the spotlight turns on.[228] Attention is a necessary ingredient for driver consciousness, but not a guarantee of it.[229]

Our attentional spotlight turns on in two ways: either through the self-driving system or deliberately by the driver. Once active, our driver takes the wheel, engaging working memory for additional processing. Think of driving in a Level 4 high-automation car. The car has a mechanism that alerts us to pay attention and decide whether to take control when it encounters a situation that may require assistance. In those moments, the car signals our attention, engaging the extra processing power of our driver to determine whether the car is taking the best course of action or whether we should provide an alternative response. Outside of those moments, we are the drivers who can direct our attention to anything we want and deliberately take control whenever we choose.

In the human vehicle, our self-driving system relies on millions of neurons that continually monitor the environment and trigger attention when something important is detected, forming what some neuroscientists refer to as the attentional filter.[230] This filter operates nonconsciously as part of our self-driving system, similar to the mechanism in a Level 4 high-automation car, alerting our conscious driver to pay extra attention.

As soon as the filter detects something important, it automatically turns on the attentional spotlight in the workspace, activating our driver to take a closer look.[231] Generally, it's on the lookout for cues related to survival or intuitive responses that may benefit from additional driver attention.[232] Once alerted, our driver can fully attend to what is in focus and take conscious control of working memory to determine whether the vehicle is making the right decision and intervene with corrective action if needed.

Often, our self-driving system signals our driver's attention, and we instantly decide that everything is fine, quickly shifting our focus elsewhere without fully engaging. These are the moments when attention can be active without full conscious awareness necessarily being engaged.

The second way our attentional spotlight becomes active is deliberately, by our driver. At any time, our driver can consciously activate attention by intentionally turning on the spotlight to take the wheel from our vehicle.[233] Once we manually activate attention with the driver, we are in control of working memory, directing its processing power toward our external or internal environment.[234] Manually controlling attention is our special power for grabbing the wheel and rising above our self-driving vehicle.

We pay attention to one thing, either through conscious decision or because our attentional filter deemed it important enough to push it to the forefront of attentional focus.[235] When attention is engaged, patterns form in the brain, and we learn. The more focused our attention is, the greater the pattern formation will be.[236]

We learn whenever the driver fully engages attention on something triggered by the filter or anything they deliberately decide to focus on in full concentration. Who we are as people is primarily determined by the attentional spotlight guiding how our network wires. As the driver, we can let our environment direct the spotlight or manually control where it shines.

Our driver circuitry is immature at birth, leaving our attention filter to select where the spotlight shines, determining how our early self-driving circuits take shape. In childhood, our executive circuitry slowly develops, giving rise to a driver who can help influence our vehicle's wiring.

As we age, our self-driving system handles most of the navigation. At the same time, our driver uses higher-level processing to guide and evaluate whether a particular decision is correct. When the driver agrees with a self-driving decision, it becomes the automatic response our vehicle uses for similar scenarios moving forward. If the driver disagrees, they can take the wheel and provide an alternative response, which may replace the original one with a new pattern to use in the future. In this way, our driver helps train our vehicle, wiring the self-driving system that will drive us in adulthood.

Through a lifetime of bumping into our environment, our driver unknowingly uses attention to wire our self-driving circuits. By our mid-to-late twenties, our driver reaches full maturity, sitting behind the wheel of a self-driving vehicle that can drive itself. Since our driver assisted in approving the automated responses that our self-driving system uses to navigate our environment, we align with them and rarely interject. For that reason, in adulthood, many of us take on a passive role, sleeping at the wheel, while our self-driving system drives with minimal supervision.

When our drivers instantly agree with self-driving decisions, they get carried out unchallenged, bypassing the scrutiny of attention, which only reinforces them further. Now, if our driver examines self-driving responses under the full scrutiny of attention and takes corrective action, that new response can replace the old one. Repeatedly correcting our self-driving system allows our driver to automate new patterns of thought and action, which rewires our vehicle.

Deliberately directing attention is how we can wake up our driver and take the wheel to challenge our vehicle. Engaging our driver more often to closely supervise our self-driving system with attention and override responses that do not serve us rewires our brain to drive with greater balance. Each of us has the potential to use our driver to overhaul our vehicle so it drives in a way that serves us.

CHAPTER 12

Applying the Brakes

Both the self-driving system and the driver in a Level 4 high-automation car use the gas, brake, and steering to drive. In either case, we are in the driver's seat, experiencing the outcome of all acceleration, braking, and steering that takes place within the vehicle. The car is the primary driver, with the most influence over the vehicle's speed and direction at any given moment, while we interact with the results of those responses.

The car handles all driving under normal conditions, and we generally take the wheel when it gets stuck or confused. As the driver, we only use the gas, brake, and steering when we are actively doing the driving; otherwise, everything we feel comes from the self-driving system. Whether we are driving or not, we are in the driver's seat, physically experiencing every move the car makes. Most of what we feel while inside the car comes from the self-driving system; it makes decisions, and we experience the outcomes.

Like a Level 4 high-automation car, the human vehicle has equivalent gas, brake, and steering controls that the self-driving system and the driver use to drive. Since we are a self-driving-first design, our vehicle handles about 80-95 percent of the driving, controlling the gas, brake, and steering during that time.[237] We are the driver making sense of the result, who is only in control, influencing our vehicle's gas, brake, and steering when consciously engaged.

The extent to which we drive versus our self-driving system is a spectrum that varies from person to person. If we are asleep at the wheel, passively agreeing with every self-driving response, our vehicle can handle up to 95 percent of the driving. On the other hand, if we actively engage our conscious driver by closely supervising the self-driving system and frequently overriding its responses, we can reduce the overall amount of driving it performs. On average, our vehicle performs about 80-95% of the driving, depending on how often we engage our conscious driver.

Our brain generates thousands of thoughts each day, most of which come from our self-driving system.[238] These arise from survival and intuitive circuits in response to external cues, as well as from the default mode when other circuits are less active. The rest of our thoughts originate from our driver circuitry when we consciously engage attention in higher-level processing.

The thoughts that result from our self-driving and driver circuits are accompanied by neurochemicals such as adrenaline, cortisol, dopamine, and serotonin, which influence our internal state.[239] Generally, negative thoughts related to stress and threats activate the sympathetic accelerator, while positive, calming thoughts tend to engage the parasympathetic brake.[240] These roughly make up the human vehicle's gas and brake that our self-driving system and driver use to drive.

When the gas is applied, our breathing speeds up, increasing our heart rate. When the brake is applied, our breathing slows, lowering our heart rate.[241] Alongside acceleration and braking, automatic motor movements can also accompany our thoughts the moment they arise. Altogether, our circuits generate thoughts that influence our internal states and external behaviors. Most of these thoughts originate from the self-driving system, making it the primary shaper of our moment-to-moment experience, while we are the driver interacting with the result.

A lifetime of experience can miscalibrate our self-driving circuits, inclining them toward negative thoughts that activate acceleration when they fire. Our survival circuits can be hypersensitive to threats. Our intuitive circuits can be limiting or destructive. Our default mode circuits can curate self-referential content that is often harmful. Research shows that a large percentage of our thoughts and core beliefs tilt toward the negative, with some estimates suggesting it could be as high as 70 percent.[242] Through a lifetime of experience, we unknowingly miscalibrate our self-driving system, making it prone to chronic acceleration. At the same time, we are the driver, locked inside, hanging on the best we can.

When driving in a Level 4 high-automation car, we are the supervisor overseeing a self-driving system. If we agree with the car's decisions, we let it drive uninterrupted, further reinforcing those responses as accurate. However, when we take the wheel from the vehicle in corrective action, either because we disagree with its decisions or it needs assistance, that correction can alter the self-driving system's programming. Information about human intervention is sent to the central office, where it's analyzed, run through simulations, and potentially added to all cars in the fleet, updating every network with that new response. Doing nothing and aligning with the self-driving system maintains the status quo, while driver intervention can reshape how it drives in the future.

Our human vehicle operates similarly. Our driver serves as the supervisor, who can either leave our self-driving decisions unchecked or take the wheel with corrective action, offering an alternative response. Our self-driving system will accelerate to give someone the finger when they cut us off, habitually scroll on our phones, or ruminate on worst-case scenarios. If we passively let these responses go unchecked, they become stronger and more likely to be used as the appropriate self-driving responses for similar scenarios in the future. It doesn't matter whether they are harmful or inaccurate; if our driver doesn't correct them, they stay the same or even get more automatic.

Many of us unknowingly spend our lives wiring a self-driving system that chronically accelerates. At the same time, we identify with these responses as accurate, rarely questioning or taking the wheel to stop them. We are meant to be the driver responsible for supervising and taking control of our self-driving system when it makes a misprediction. That rarely happens because we are unaware of our role as supervisors. We agree with most of the self-driving system's suggestions, almost sleeping at the wheel as our vehicle drives uninterrupted.[243] We align with a self-driving system that can drive recklessly, and without corrective driver action, it never changes.

Unlike in a Level 4 high-automation car, when we override our self-driving system with our driver, a new neural pattern can form in real time to represent that correction. Thanks to neuroplasticity, where attention goes, neural patterns grow, and if we do not use a pattern, we lose it.

Deliberately activating the attentional spotlight with our driver allows us to take control of the vehicle and consciously assess what it is doing in that moment. If we determine that the self-driving response is inaccurate and is unnecessarily accelerating, our driver can take the wheel and override the vehicle to apply the brakes instead.

When our conscious driver steps in and takes an alternative action, we prevent the self-driving system from fully firing its stored pattern, which weakens it. At the same time, by using attention to take a different action, we fire a new pattern in its place, which, with repetition, becomes automatic.[244] In this way, when our driver deliberately uses attention to interrupt the vehicle's acceleration and apply the brakes instead, we replace responses that do not serve us with new ones. Over time, this allows us to retrain our self-driving system to drive with greater balance.

One way to wake up our driver and take the wheel to override our self-driving system is through deliberate, conscious control of our breath. We breathe roughly 20,000 times a day, and our breathing rate shifts as we accelerate and brake.[245] Inhalation tends to be associated with sympathetic acceleration, while exhalation is associated with the parasympathetic brake.[246] When the sympathetic accelerator is active, we breathe in faster, increasing our heart rate. On the other hand, when the parasympathetic brake is active, we breathe out more slowly, decreasing our heart rate.[247]

For the most part, our self-driving system automatically controls our breathing outside of our awareness. How we breathe reflects how our self-driving system is wired. If our self-driving circuits are well-calibrated, then we will likely breathe in a controlled, balanced manner. However, if our self-driving system is miscalibrated and constantly accelerating, our breathing will likely become more rapid and unbalanced. Our self-driving system manages our breath in the background, and we grow so accustomed to it that we do not even notice.

Once an acceleration event has passed, the self-driving system automatically triggers our parasympathetic brake to restore balance. Our parasympathetic brake's ability to bring our breathing, heart rate, and other bodily functions back to baseline after acceleration relies mainly on the vagus nerve.[248] The vagus nerve connects the brain to the body, enabling our self-driving system to activate rest and digestion by slowing the breath and decreasing our heart rate.[249] This braking mechanism is managed directly by the self-driving system, which is generally engaged after acceleration to return us to baseline.

If our self-driving circuits are miscalibrated, they chronically trigger acceleration in the background, making it difficult for our vehicle to keep us balanced with the brakes. Through no fault of our own, our breathing reflects that imbalance, while we are the driver, doing our best to hang on. Fortunately, we can consciously control our breath, and that is where our true power lies.

Deliberately controlling our breath with our driver allows us to apply the brakes and slow down whenever our vehicle accelerates. By consciously going to our breath and exhaling slowly, we can intentionally stimulate the vagus nerve and activate the parasympathetic brake.[250] Slow, deliberate breathing is the secret power that lets us take the wheel with our driver and apply the brakes whenever we choose.

When our miscalibrated self-driving circuits trigger worry, fear, anger, frustration, shame, guilt, or anxiety, we can turn to our breath and manually apply the brakes. By breathing slowly, we interrupt these self-driving responses, stimulate the vagus nerve, and activate the parasympathetic brake while easing off the accelerator.[251] Each of us can deliberately use our breath to slow down anytime our self-driving system speeds up.

By interrupting acceleration to apply the brake instead, our driver can tune our self-driving system to accelerate less for a particular response. Each time we override acceleration with the brake, we help rewire the self-driving system toward greater balance. Deliberately focusing on slow breathing with driver attention allows us to press the brake and recalibrate our self-driving circuitry to drive with ease.

CHAPTER 13

External Relief

The human Level 4 high-automation vehicle is always on and running in the background, continuously determining our momentary states. Our self-driving system is the primary driver, influencing our gas, brake, and steering every second our driver is not consciously engaged at the wheel. The way our vehicle drives is shaped by its internal wiring, honed over a lifetime of experience. If our self-driving circuits are miscalibrated, our vehicle can be prone to acceleration, driving with a heavy foot. It will chronically slam on the gas, press hard on the brakes, and steer sharply while we are locked inside, experiencing the result.

We are the drivers who often label automatic self-driving responses associated with acceleration as painful emotions, such as boredom, frustration, anxiety, shame, anger, guilt, worry, regret, and resentment. Each of these emotions carries its own unique neurochemical signature, typically linked to sympathetic activation, while we, as the driver, interact with the outcome, often appraising it as pain.

If miscalibrated, our self-driving system will routinely trigger acceleration responses outside our awareness, creating a backdrop of pain that we experience as the driver. It's like riding in a Level 4 high-automation car that's trained to drive aggressively, constantly slamming on the gas. As the driver, we have no say in how the self-driving system drives; we simply experience the result. When our human vehicle's self-driving system is miscalibrated, it accelerates uncontrollably, while we, the conscious driver, experience the outcome as pain and struggle to maintain control.

To alleviate the underlying pain caused by the acceleration of our self-driving system, we often engage in external activities that bring pleasure or relaxation. Drinking coffee, shopping, playing video games, gambling, and scrolling social media typically activate sympathetic acceleration linked to pleasure. Watching TV, eating comfort food, drinking alcohol, and consuming cannabis are activities that tend to engage the parasympathetic brake, providing relaxation. Each of these activities has distinct neurochemical signatures tied to pleasure or relaxation that temporarily shift us away from painful acceleration.

It does not matter what external activities we use to relieve painful acceleration; none of them are personal. When we first engage in a pleasurable or relaxing activity, there is no existing pattern in the brain to represent it. When we play a video game, scroll through social media, or watch TV for the first time, we engage our attention, and a pattern begins to form. We like how it feels, so we repeat the activity, firing the pattern again and tuning it further until it eventually becomes an automatic function. Once automated, the activity is available to either the self-driving system, which can trigger it based on subtle cues, or to the driver, who can use it at their discretion.

By adulthood, we are behind the wheel of a self-driving system that we have unknowingly stockpiled with automatic behaviors that it uses to relieve the painful acceleration it generates. Bored, we watch TV; tired, we drink coffee; anxious, we smoke a joint, that's certainly how my vehicle's wired to respond. These responses aren't personal; they're simply automated outputs, wired through a lifetime of experience, that our self-driving system automatically executes to escape discomfort.

These pleasurable and relaxing responses do not last forever. If our self-driving circuits are miscalibrated, the vehicle inevitably returns to its baseline of painful acceleration. When that happens, our self-driving system will once again trigger its available external strategies to relieve the pain. Our vehicle falls into a perpetual loop where it produces pain and repeatedly engages in the same automated actions in an attempt to relieve it.

As the driver, we experience the results of these self-driving, pleasurable, or relaxing decisions only after they happen. In most cases, our driver doesn't notice, aligns completely, or finds them too difficult to override, and the self-driving response wins out. None of it is really our fault; our self-driving vehicle is powerful, and we've never been shown how to take control and overpower it with our driver.

There's no reason to get upset when we act against what we consciously want. It is simply an impersonal self-driving system using wired external behaviors to escape the pain it creates, all outside our awareness. Yet, we personalize these self-driving responses, becoming frustrated because we can't seem to gain control of our vehicle. In reality, that frustration only adds to the pain, prompting the self-driving system to trigger even more of its pain-relieving strategies.

A common strategy people use to escape pain is to deliberately divert their attention to external activities that benefit them, such as exercise, reading, painting, or playing an instrument or a sport. These are activities that require mental effort and are less prone to automation, especially in the early stages, but they carry pleasurable or relaxing signatures when we engage in them. My personal favorites are listening to audiobooks, working out, and writing.

As the driver, we can manually force ourselves to engage in these beneficial external activities whenever we want. The challenge is that they only provide short-term relief until our self-driving system resumes driving and returns to its baseline of painful acceleration. Although audiobooks, working out, and writing were beneficial for me, they did not permanently resolve the underlying pain associated with my miscalibrated circuits.

By deliberately using our driver to focus attention on beneficial activities, we come close to the answer that can help us feel better once and for all. The challenge is that while these activities can strengthen the brain in valuable ways, they remain external behaviors and do not fully address the internal wiring that fuels the self-driving responses underlying our pain.

Attention is the key to rewiring our brains for greater balance, but the most profound changes come when we turn it inward.

That's where the real transformation happens, where we go under the hood, challenge our self-driving system with our driver, and rewire it at the source. Do that, and we not only feel better in the moment; we also improve our vehicle's performance for the rest of our lives.

CHAPTER 14

Moving Inward with Mindfulness

What if the answer to relieving painful acceleration is not external and outside of us, but where we instinctively avoid: inside?

We naturally resist looking inward, but it is the best way to go under the hood and rewire our self-driving system at its source for lasting change. Deliberately directing our attention internally toward our breath is how our driver can take the wheel and engage the brake whenever we want.

Once we gain control of the vehicle and slow it down, we can consciously question the validity of our self-driving responses without being swept away by them, asking ourselves:

- What is this emotion?
- What is it telling me?
- Where do I feel it?
- What are the sensations that accompany it?

Looking internally and asking questions is how we use our driver to intervene with self-driving responses to challenge their validity. Generally, with plasticity, what we fire we wire, and what we do not use we lose. When we align with self-driving responses and let them go unchecked, we only reinforce them further.

By deliberately directing attention inward toward the breath, we engage the conscious driver and seize control of our vehicle. When we do that, we activate our driver circuitry while quieting the self-driving circuits that are firing. Every time we take the wheel with our driver by directing attention to the breath, we strengthen our executive circuits, while gradually weakening the self-driving responses we interrupt. With repetition, our driver can deliberately turn inward with attention and overhaul our self-driving system to drive in ways that serve us.

The difficulty with going inward is that if we are not used to engaging our driver and challenging our self-driving system in that way, our driver is underdeveloped, making it extremely difficult for them to take control of our vehicle. Going internal to rewire our self-driving system requires us to train and strengthen our driver so they can remain in power without being overthrown by our vehicle. Once our driver circuitry is strong enough to take the wheel and stay in control, we can use it to deliberately override self-driving decisions that do not serve us, recalibrating our vehicle to drive with greater balance.

I have spent the last five years using my driver to go inward, experiencing some success as I attempt to rewire my self-driving system, but I am far from complete. I have successfully recalibrated and altered many automatic responses relating to fear, anxiety, and anger. At the same time, those tied to habits like coffee or cannabis remain more challenging for me to change. After engaging in coffee and cannabis chronically for years without gaining an edge, I am now able to go long periods without them. However, as soon as I use them again, I fall right back into the same self-driving cycles of escapism.

Either way, wherever we are, it's all progress on the path of rewiring the brain. Taking the wheel and overriding a behavior is a win, but even noticing a behavior after it happens is also a win. We are self-driving first, so naturally, we are going to engage in the behaviors and thoughts we want to avoid before we can successfully prevent them entirely.

Early on, simply noticing our self-driving responses and having an open dialogue with them is critical. Try not to take these impersonal reactions personally. It's essential to reset expectations: it has taken many years to wire our brains the way they are, and it may take many more to rewire them the way we want with our driver. There are no quick fixes when it comes to rewiring our brains. Some changes can happen quickly, but deeply miscalibrated circuits may take many years of repeated failure to recalibrate and bring them into balance.

When considering rewiring our brains, it may help to think of it as learning a physical skill to mastery. Like any skill, it may take thousands of hours of deliberate practice to wire our mental muscles to self-mastery, and most of the time, progress feels invisible. Think of looking inward with our driver to challenge our self-driving responses as the mental training required to overhaul the neural network that drives us. It will not happen overnight, but taking the wheel and internally exploring automatic responses with attention is how each of us can rewire the self-driving system with our driver.

Over 2,500 years ago, the Buddha unknowingly introduced the ultimate internal workout for rewiring the brain: mindfulness meditation.[252] Even bhāvanā, the traditional term we translate as meditation, means "development through mental training."[253]

Mindfulness is not strictly a spiritual practice; it is a mental training tool available to anyone that we can use to turn inward and rewire our brains at the source.[254] Supported by growing research, thousands of doctors, therapists, and counselors now regularly recommend mindfulness as a powerful resource for healing.[255] Today, mindfulness remains as relevant as ever, serving as both a mental training exercise to strengthen our driver circuitry and a roadmap for going under the hood to recalibrate our self-driving system.

Mindfulness training consists of two components. The first is strengthening the driver's attention circuits so we can take the wheel from our vehicle and stay in control without it overpowering us. Once we train our driver to do that successfully, the next step is to use that position to actively challenge and override automatic responses that do not serve us, to rewire our self-driving system.[256] First, we must strengthen our attention so we can seize control of the vehicle and remain steady at the wheel with our driver. When they are strong enough, we can use them to rewire the self-driving system through corrective action.

At its core, mindfulness is a concentration practice that involves deliberately directing our attention spotlight onto a neutral anchor and sustaining it for as long as we can.[257] There are many forms available, including sitting meditation, walking meditation, yoga, and centering prayers.[258] Each method involves deliberately placing full attention on a repetitive anchor, such as a word, a prayer, a bodily sensation, or a movement.[259]

Attention roughly equates to driver activation. Deliberately focusing attention on an anchor in mindfulness activates our driver at the wheel. Every time we place our focus on an anchor, we gain control of the self-driving system and remain there until our attention fades. In that way, anchors provide a neutral, stable space where we can momentarily seize control of our vehicle with our driver, apply the brake, and get relief from our self-driving system at any time.[260]

One of the most common anchors in mindfulness is the breath, which involves consciously attending to the act of breathing, especially by slowing it down.[261] When we place our attention on our breath and control our breathing, we are taking the wheel from the vehicle with our driver. At the same time, breathing slowly and in a controlled manner, especially on exhalation, activates the parasympathetic brake.

All day long, the self-driving system regulates our breathing automatically, outside our awareness. If our self-driving circuits are miscalibrated, they may continually trigger acceleration, and our breathing will follow. Usually, we are the drivers experiencing the result, doing our best to cope. Mindful breathing brings us back into our bodies and into the present moment, where we can take control of the vehicle and apply the brakes to slow down at any time.[262]

We are the drivers of a self-driving vehicle that has never been told how to take control and apply the brakes. Without that knowledge, most people, myself included, spend much of their lives asleep at the wheel, with the driver disengaged as the self-driving system drives unchallenged, with minimal supervision. Mindfulness is the key to engaging our driver and taking control of our vehicle so we can drive the way we want.

Since our drivers have been disengaged and sleeping for so long, the first phase of mindfulness involves waking them up and strengthening their ability to maintain control of the vehicle.[263] Each time we place our attention on the breath, we engage our driver. At the same time, sustaining our attention on the breath exercises our attention circuits and strengthens our driver's ability to remain in control of the vehicle.[264]

In the early stages of mindfulness, our driver is weak and undertrained, so it is normal for our attention to drift within seconds of attending to our breath. The moment attention fades, the self-driving system will resume control, filling our minds with thoughts from our survival, intuitive, and default mode circuits. When we notice that we have lost attention and the self-driving system has kicked in, the instruction is simple: deliberately place our focus back on our breath to engage the driver and take the wheel once again.

Think of the first phase of mindfulness as mental training that conditions our driver to take and stay in control of our vehicle. Each time we place attention on our breath, realize we have lost focus, and return attention to our breathing, it’s one rep. Like physical training, it's going to take thousands of reps to build our driver's mental muscle. Holding concentration on the anchor and continually bringing our focus back to it when it strays is mental conditioning for our driver's attention circuitry.[265] The longer we can hold our attention, the longer we can stay in control.

At first, the driver is no match for the self-driving system, and maintaining focus feels impossible. But even noticing when we've lost attention is a form of progress. Over time, with each rep, we strengthen our attention circuits and improve our ability to remain in control of the vehicle. With enough practice, we can train our driver to take the wheel from the self-driving system and remain unmoved as we stay anchored in attention. The goal of the first phase is to condition our driver's attention circuits so we can take and maintain control of our vehicle whenever we choose.

Another benefit of the first phase of mindfulness is that every time we deliberately place our attention on our breathing and slow our breath, we are not only taking the wheel as the driver, but also applying the brakes.[266] Longer exhalations activate the vagus nerve, triggering the parasympathetic relaxation response that helps relieve stress and restore balance.[267] Each slow in-and-out breath we take moves us away from stress mode and into relaxation mode.[268] That makes mindfulness a practical way for the driver to apply the brakes and trigger relaxation anytime the vehicle accelerates. Over time, repeated interruption of stress-based acceleration with our driver can recalibrate our self-driving system.

Research now links mindfulness to measurable improvements in physical and mental well-being. It boosts immune function and helps regulate blood pressure and cortisol levels. At the same time, it reduces anxiety, depression, and emotional reactivity.[269] Every second we spend in mindfulness is additional time spent in relaxation mode, helping to rebalance and heal our human vehicle.

The first phase of mindfulness training is about strengthening our attention so we can take and stay in control of our vehicle with our driver whenever we want. Once we are proficient at activating our driver behind the wheel, the second phase is using them to override and rewire our self-driving system in ways that serve us. When we start to impartially observe automatic responses with our driver, we gain new insights that challenge our thinking and alter the brain's wiring.

When riding in a Level 4 high-automation car, there is a clear separation between the driver and the self-driving system. Nothing the car does is personal. If at any time the vehicle gets stuck or we don't like what it's doing, we can grab the wheel and take corrective action. There would be no confusion between responses that come from us or the car.

In the human vehicle, on the other hand, it is not so easy to distinguish ourselves from the self-driving system because we become so accustomed to it. After a lifetime spent in our vehicle, we no longer notice that the two systems work as one, as we personalize every automatic response as our own.

Our self-driving system will tell us not to meditate, yell when our favorite team is losing, panic when we think we've lost our wallet, slam a door in frustration, worry about death from a random pain, drink coffee when we're tired, or say we are too old or too young to do something. We often instantly identify with these responses without a second thought, not realizing they are automatic, conditioned, and usually inaccurate. The reality is that most of our responses originate from the self-driving system and are separate from us.

The first phase of mindfulness is about developing our driver at the wheel as a separate entity that can take control of the self-driving system. Once we have that separation, we move on to the second phase of mindfulness training, where we use our driver to question our vehicle's responses without attachment and override what does not serve us, just as we would if we were driving a Level 4 high-automation car.

Anytime we deliberately anchor our attention on the breath in mindfulness, we take control of our vehicle with our driver. Once anchored in the breath, we can mindfully observe self-driving responses without attachment by placing our attention on the energy that accompanies them rather than their storyline. When we focus on the sensations behind our thoughts rather than the narratives they carry, we find they often dissolve quickly into nothingness. In the second phase of mindfulness, we anchor in attention, taking the wheel with our driver, and observe thoughts, emotions, and sensations without judgment as they come and go.[270] We are teaching ourselves that we are separate from our self-driving system, and we do not have to idly follow every suggestion it makes.

Emotions continually rise and fall throughout the day, and they may not be designed to last as long as we have come to know. Some mindfulness teachers suggest that the physical sensations that accompany an emotion may even pass after about

90 seconds when not fully fueled by thought.[271] As an experiment, try interrupting an emotion when it arises by counting to 90 and see how long it lasts.

When we attach to the story behind emotions, we fuel their energy, which can make them last for what feels like hours. But when viewed mindfully, the self-driving circuits responsible for that energy tend to quiet down, and the emotion can quickly fade. Interacting with the energy behind our self-driving responses, rather than attaching to the story they carry, can lead to insights that shift our relationship with them and rewire our brains.[272]

Instead of instantly attaching to our vehicle's prompt to drink coffee, check our phone, or yell in rage, we can override it by anchoring in our breath to observe the energy behind the automatic suggestion. When we do that, the energy underlying these responses dissolves, and we expose them, realizing they may not be as real as we have come to know. When we can remain unmoved by our self-driving responses, watching as they come and go, we gain a new perspective and power over our vehicle. Slowly, we begin to understand that our self-driving responses are not personal and don't define us; with mindfulness, we are in control.

Intentionally interrupting automatic reactions with mindfulness loosens the grip of the old circuitry and strengthens pathways for new self-driving responses. In the second phase of mindfulness, we actively involve our driver to challenge our self-driving system and reshape our internal wiring, one response at a time, so our vehicle drives more smoothly.

We're waking up from automaticity by using deliberate attention to go under the hood with our driver and overhaul our self-driving system.[273] It's the process of intentionally engaging our driver to question our self-driving system and discard what no longer serves us, as we retrain our vehicle to drive with greater balance.[274]

Mindfulness training is a powerful tool for building attention, applying the brake, and rewiring our self-driving circuits. But like any skill, it takes time, and we likely won't see results overnight. Rewiring the brain is a slow, deliberate process. Mastering both elements of mindfulness may take years, and the work is never truly done.

CHAPTER 15

Mindfulness Instruction

Mindfulness is the secret to awakening our driver within by using deliberate attention to take the wheel from our self-driving system and rewire it for greater balance. Now we just have to learn how to do it and begin our mental training. Just as we go to the gym for physical exercise, our driver must enter our mental gym to exercise their mind. We do this by establishing a stable position to anchor ourselves in so our driver can move inward and train our attention circuits through mindfulness.

The traditional image that comes to mind when thinking of mindfulness is a person sitting with their eyes closed, cross-legged in the half-lotus position.[275] Closing our eyes in a seated position helps shut out much of the external world by decreasing the amount of sensory input that flows into the brain, which reduces the activation of cue-dependent circuits. Sensory information can still enter and trigger these circuits, but the position limits their activity, keeping them relatively quiet while we meditate.

For the most part, grounding in a position provides a controlled environment that reduces the activity of survival and intuitive circuits, creating a mental arena where our driver can primarily contend with the default mode circuitry. Generally, when we lose focus, the mind wanders, and we simply return attention to the breath. With repetition, we strengthen our attention and improve our driver's ability to take the wheel.

The lotus position isn't an absolute requirement; sitting in a chair, lying down, standing, or even walking are all valid options, especially when we are just starting out.[276] Early on, anchoring on stable ground is more important because we want to quiet the mind; it's ok to prioritize comfort over tradition. If a position is too demanding, it can cause sensory overload and overstimulate our cue-dependent circuits, making it even more challenging to stay grounded in attention.

Trying movements or exercises that are too advanced when we're physically working out for the first time may push us past our limits and make us give up before we even give them a chance. Similarly with mental training, if the position we choose is too demanding, it may turn us off mindfulness entirely.

Starting with a simple, comfortable position is ideal because it effectively blocks externals, allowing us to move inward and strengthen our attention while keeping the difficulty level low. Later, as we become more proficient, we can experiment with new positions and deepen our practice further.

Once we've established our position and close our eyes, we are ready to anchor in the breath. Start by inhaling through the nose for a count of five, breathing deeply from the belly, then exhaling through the mouth for an equal or longer duration.[277] The goal is to follow this breathing pattern whenever we are practicing mindfulness.

Although we focus on breathing in a specific rhythm when being mindful, it is usually not enough on its own to sustain our attention, so complementary anchors can be added to help. We can silently say "breathing in" and "breathing out" with each inhale and exhale.[278] Or we can concentrate on all the sensations of breathing, from feeling the air move through our nostrils and out of our mouth, to the rise and fall of the belly.[279] Whatever helps sustain attention is best, and part of the mental training is experimenting to find what works.

My favorite anchor is a 2,600-year-old technique shared by Thich Nhat Hanh that gamifies mindfulness by turning it into a concentration-based counting game. As we breathe, count each combined inhalation and subsequent exhalation as one. Start from zero, trying to reach ten and back without losing count. When we do lose count, simply start from the beginning and try again. Continue that way for the entire mindfulness session, seeing how far we can get before attention fades.[280]

It is a concentration game meant to train our driver's attention. When first starting, don't be surprised if we only get to three before losing count. If ten is too difficult, try going to five instead, and increase to ten when it becomes easier. After a few months to a year of practice, we will get further in our count and eventually reach ten and back without losing focus.

Reaching a higher count over time allows us to measure our progress and track improvement as continued practice slowly strengthens our driver's attention circuits. The further we get in our count, the stronger our driver becomes, and the better we get at taking the wheel from the self-driving system.

Regardless of the anchor we choose, our attention will inevitably fade. If our cue-dependent circuits are quiet, the default mode circuits kick in, generating wandering thoughts. In the first phase of mindfulness, the goal is to notice when we lose focus and the mind is wandering, label it "thinking," and return to our anchor.[281] It sounds easy, but in the early stages of training, our driver is undeveloped and so accustomed to mind-wandering that we won't even recognize when it's happening. We may think we are focused and mindful, but in reality, we spend most of the session in default mode.[282]

The counting game is excellent because it makes losing focus more obvious. When we lose count, we know attention is lost, and we're likely in mind-wandering mode. We don't attach to the wandering thoughts; we just notice that we lost count and start again. With that, we begin to expose our self-driving system, revealing the true nature of our minds and how automatic it really is.

If we are new to mindfulness, we apply the above instruction to the first phase, where the focus is on strengthening our attention circuits to improve our driver's ability to take the wheel and stay in control of the vehicle. Deliberately anchoring in our breath, losing focus, and returning attention to our breathing repeatedly is the work that strengthens our driver. Eventually, with enough practice, we can bulk up our driver's attention circuitry to the point where we can take the wheel and remain in control at any time. The self-driving system remains powerful and often gets its way, but strengthening our driver increases our chances of seizing control.

Once we've built up our driver sufficiently in the first phase, which can take months to years of practice, we can move on to the second phase of mindfulness. In this phase, we anchor in mindfulness, engaging our driver at the wheel to challenge our self-driving responses through non-attachment and rewire our vehicle to drive with greater balance.

We do that by changing what we anchor our attention on. In the first phase, we focus on the sensations of breathing; in the second phase, we turn our attention to the sensations that accompany our thoughts as they arise.[283] Rather than instantly returning to our breath once we notice our attention has faded, the next phase involves placing attention on the energy behind the thoughts that emerge.[284] Well-known mindfulness expert Pema Chödrön's instruction is to "*drop the storyline and find the feeling.*"[285]

During meditation and in daily life, the self-driving system continuously generates thoughts that carry energy. These suggestions tell us to stop meditating, drink coffee, ruminate on an argument, scream when someone cuts us off, or worry about worst-case scenarios. Usually, our driver attaches to the story behind these responses, accepting them as accurate, which only fuels them further.

Dropping the story and going to the energy is a different approach that can effectively neutralize self-driving responses.[286] Rather than associating with our thoughts, we direct our attention inward and search our bodies for the energy they bring, exploring qualities like heat, tightness, tingling, or pressure. We're not suppressing these thoughts; we're embracing them by mindfully accepting their full energy without attachment, to fully expose the truth behind them.[287]

When we attend to the sensations behind our thoughts in this way, the initial thought lifts, and the energy it carries dissipates. One second, a self-driving response to stop meditating, drink coffee, or yell seems impossible to resist, and the next, it is gone, while we remain unmoved. When that happens, we self-liberate, gaining insight and detaching from the power of the self-driving thoughts that drive us.[288]

Mindfully attending to feelings creates a critical distance that allows us to take corrective action with our driver, without being carried away by our self-driving system.[289] Focusing on the sensations in the second phase is our driver's ability to impartially question and override our vehicle's automatic responses.

Regularly interrupting self-driving responses by mindfully going to the energy with our driver enables us to take hold of our mind and rewire it to what we want.[290] Each time we drop the story and deliberately place attention on the energy, we activate our driver circuitry, which neutralizes and quiets the initial self-driving response. Repeatedly disrupting a particular self-driving reaction in this manner can wire it to be more neutral.

Consider if our self-driving system triggers a sympathetic acceleration response. If we attach to it, the vehicle will continue to accelerate uninterrupted. However, if we place all our attention on the sensations behind it, we engage the driver, who interrupts the self-driving acceleration response and applies the brakes instead.

Repeatedly neutralizing specific self-driving acceleration responses with our driver by going to the energy can rewire them to accelerate less when they fire. Using this approach to target particular thoughts and behaviors prone to acceleration enables our driver to overhaul our self-driving system to drive with greater balance. Dropping the story and focusing on the energy in the second phase allows anyone to rewire their vehicle however they want.

Rewiring our brains through mindfulness is available to everyone, but it takes many years of effort. Similar to physical exercise, we must practice regularly to achieve results and maintain mental fitness. To successfully rewire our self-driving system, we must practice formally for fixed periods and informally throughout the day as we interact with the world.

Formal practice is helpful for both phases of mindfulness. In the first phase, it is ideal for exercising attention circuits; in the second, it provides a safe space to explore the energy behind thoughts that arise. Every second of formal mindfulness, whether it is 10, 20, or 30 minutes, is time spent in our mental gym, strengthening our attention and rewiring our circuits.

Formal meditation involves anchoring in a position for a fixed period, creating an ideal environment for our driver to contend with our default mode circuits. Every time we notice mind-wandering and return to the breath in the first phase, we tip the balance toward our executive circuitry. In the second phase, we attend to the sensations behind our wandering thoughts, diffuse them to see the truth, and recalibrate those circuits at the source.

We must intervene with self-driving survival, intuitive, and default mode responses in mindfulness if we want to alter their wiring. Since we limit external stimuli during formal mindfulness, our survival and intuitive circuits are less active than when we're living our lives, leaving many of those responses untouched during formal practice. To really address our self-driving cue-dependent circuits, we need to informally visit them in mindfulness as we move through our environment, when they are most active.[291]

In daily life, our self-driving system triggers habits, anger, frustration, fear, or anxiety, initially outside our awareness, and we attach to them without a second thought. They tell us what to approach or avoid, like or hate, and we rarely challenge them. Informal mindfulness is how we use our driver in real time to take the wheel from our self-driving system and intervene with its responses.

If we have a miscalibrated self-driving system, it can chronically trigger acceleration in response to much of what we encounter. Informal mindfulness allows us to take control and apply the brake whenever we want. In the first phase, we can intervene by deliberately placing our attention on our breath, and in the second phase, we can go to the energy. Either way, we are taking control of our self-driving system and overriding it with our driver. With repetition, we recalibrate the circuits underlying that particular response. Using mindfulness informally throughout the day allows us to strategically intervene in automatic reactions as they happen, rewiring our self-driving system for greater balance.[292]

Together, formal and informal mindfulness practices strengthen our driver at the wheel, allowing us to strategically engage them to rewire our self-driving system in ways that serve us. Training our driver with mindfulness to recalibrate our brains is a proven strategy available to anyone willing to put in the work. Nothing happens overnight, but with persistent practice, the brain will respond; that is all it knows.

Now that we understand the human vehicle and how to engage the driver within to rewire our self-driving system, the next part of the book dives deeper into the brain as a network, fully explaining how it uses plasticity to unbiasedly form functional patterns through experience. It starts with understanding our network, made of neuron computers and the support cells that maintain them, as they cohabitate to manufacture our reality. After that, we take a peek at artificial networks to explain how information flowing through patterns leads to function. From there, we return to the human neural network and examine how the unbiased process of plasticity impartially shapes our brain based on what we think and do the most, shaping the automatic functions that drive us.

PART 2

Networks and Human Potential

CHAPTER 16

Neurons

Humanity's greatest challenge is understanding how the brain works.[293] With discoveries in neuroscience and artificial intelligence, we are inching closer to this answer each day. While its full functionality remains a mystery, it is now commonly understood that the brain is a living network whose collective activity gives rise to our human experience.

The brain generates thousands of thoughts daily, and we're so caught up in the outcome that we rarely consider the effort of our cells to create them.[294] Within our brain is a bustling community of 86 billion neurons and 85 billion support cells.[295] Protected by the blood-brain barrier, these two categories of cells work together harmoniously, forming the biological cellular network that produces our thoughts and actions.

Neurons, the building blocks of our brain, first appeared in species between 635 and 540 million years ago.[296] From worms to humans, they have similar designs and functions wherever they live. The differences between humans and other animals with neurons lie in the number, regions, connectivity, and configuration of those neurons.

Our neurons are a community of cells living in a cellular world, experiencing life and death just as we do. Each one is a signaling unit with the same general function. They accumulate a charge and fire an electric spike once a specific threshold is reached. It's similar to getting a static shock. Our body builds up a charge, and when it reaches a certain potential, a spike of energy is released from our finger.

When a neuron is at rest, its total charge is -70 millivolts, and it only fires when it reaches +40 millivolts.[297] As soon as it builds up a charge, reaching the firing threshold, it discharges an electrical spike and resets to -70 millivolts to repeat the process. The brain is filled with neurons that generate spikes and release chemicals. They typically fire between 5 and 50 times per second, though some may fire faster or slower depending on the type.[298]

Each neuron comes into the world as an independent entity that lives to fire electrochemical signals with others. They are individuals performing jobs that, when combined, contribute to how we think and feel. The activity of billions of individual neurons, firing signals in patterns as a collective unit, leads to thought and reality as we know it. *Every thought you have is the activity of neurons. Everything you see, hear, or feel is also the activity of neurons. Our mental states and the activity of neurons are one and the same.*[299]

Although there are many different types of neurons, they all share the same general layout, with an input for receiving, a body for processing, and an output for sending signals. The input is made of one to several thousand fibrous branches, each filled with granular spines that receive signals from neighboring neurons.[300] These input branches and spines are highly malleable, growing and withering in response to activity. The signals received at the input determine whether a positive or negative charge enters the cell body.

The body is where incoming charge flows and where the electrical spike is generated once the firing threshold is reached. The cell body is the control center that processes information and manages signaling.[301] The spike the cell body produces shoots down its output cable of varying lengths, ranging from microscopic to three feet long.[302] The signal travels up to 270 miles per hour along the output cable, covering more than the length of a football field in one second.[303]

Once the electric charge reaches the end of the cable, it triggers the release of chemicals known as neurotransmitters that flow to neighboring neurons. Common neurotransmitters include dopamine, serotonin, glutamate, and GABA.[304] These chemicals shower thousands of neighboring cells and influence whether they fire.

Neurons are most often arranged in layers, with the ends of output cables pointing at the input connections of neurons in the next layer to promote optimal signal transfer. The outputs and inputs are separated by one-millionth of a centimeter, connecting at the synapse but never directly touching.[305] Synapses are how neurons communicate, acting as connection points that transfer chemicals from the output of one neuron to the input of another.

Each neuron has thousands to tens of thousands of synaptic connection points for transferring chemicals. They grow and wither away based on use, as neural activity influences their behavior. Altogether, the brain has roughly 100 trillion synaptic connections that coordinate signal transfer between neurons.[306]

Neurons are not simple on-and-off switches but complex agents that continually manage input signals and generate spikes every second of the day.[307] Rather than switches, they function more like computers that process information and communicate with many others. Instead of being a single giant computer, the brain is a network with an average of 86 billion computers that send signals in complex patterns to produce the projection of reality we experience.

CHAPTER 17

Support Cells

Our neurons are highly interconnected computers that receive, process, and transmit electrochemical impulses. The output cables run here and there, connecting every neuron in some way to form an intricate network that supports the communication of 86 billion computers. Such an extensive, complex network needs help to function properly; that is where the other 85 billion cells in our brain come in.[308]

These are our support cells, acting as the brain's network technicians. At least seven types of these cellular workers manage signal transfer in the brain.[309] Together, they service all the neuron computers and their connecting cables to ensure optimal signal transfer throughout the brain. The network technicians are the supporting cast taking care of the infrastructure that carries our neural traffic. Neurons and their output cables form a complex network, while support cells help keep it operational.

The support cells also play a unique role in managing signal speed on the output cables. One type, oligodendrocytes, adds a fatty insulation to the cables that fire most often, enabling them to send signals faster.[310] Daniel Coyle, the author of *The Talent*

Code, calls them broadband installers because they improve signal speed on every output cable they touch.

They all have the same design, acting as rogue sentinels with 10-20 tentacle-like extensions that attach to surrounding cables as they float through the cellular space of our brain.[311] Their tentacles contact a segment of an output cable, where they install a performance-enhancing fatty material called myelin. The ends of the extensions excrete myelin in layers, wrapping around a 0.1-millimeter-wide section of cable 40-50 times over days and weeks.[312]

The entire cable is not wrapped at once; instead, myelin is added on small segments that end up looking like sausages after the fatty substance is installed. When every section of a cable is fully wrapped with myelin, it resembles a string of sausages, having a small gap between each one.[313] The broadband installers have 10-20 extremities that connect to surrounding cables, making speed-boosting fat sausages on every section of cable they touch. They are cellular sausage makers moving through the brain, serving an area of 20, 30, 40, or even 50 neighboring cables.[314]

A bare cable sends signals up to 20 mph, but when it is fully myelinated, with a whole string of sausages, speeds can reach 270 mph.[315] By strategically adding "sausages" to cables that fire the most, our broadband installers increase signal speeds and firing rates, boosting overall information processing between neurons by up to 3,000 times.[316] This strategic enhancement empowers us to improve at what we do the most.

When we are born, most of our neurons lay bare because they are relatively new, and our activity-dependent installers have not yet had the chance to add myelin to them. As we age and neurons fire through experience, our broadband installers are sent out in waves of millions to improve the cables that send the most signals.

By the time we are adults, there is a myelin footprint of cables we unknowingly tune through experience, shaping how we see the world. In adulthood, we are the culmination of what we have done the most, as myelin has been obediently working in the background to tune our reality.

The broadband installers are unbiased, activity-driven sentinels that go where the action is. To them, there is no good or bad; all they know is to add myelin to the cables that fire the most. When we say we can't do something, we're saying that the installers will not add myelin, which is all they know to do. They do not care who you are; they work the same way in everyone.

If we do something enough, regardless of what it is, specific neurons fire and the installers add myelin, improving our proficiency. The broadband installers will make us the best at what we think and do the most, no questions asked. We can make myelin work for us and achieve anything we desire at any time in our lives. Just grab the wheel with attention and take action; myelin will do the rest.

CHAPTER 18

Understanding Networks

To understand the relationship between neurons and support cells, it helps to think of an internet service provider connecting computers over a network of interconnected cables. Every computer that is connected processes information and communicates over the network, while the network technicians keep it all operational.

Our brain has 86 billion neurons, each of which can be thought of as a single computer that receives, processes, and sends signals to many others through a labyrinth of output cables that connect them all. Every neuron connects with others, forming complex circuits that enable them to integrate information and communicate. Our roughly 85 billion support cells are the network technicians who maintain the infrastructure and manage signal transfer between our neuron computers. Neurons and support cells form a biological network that works together harmoniously to generate the reality we experience.

The brain is not one computer, but a living network made of 86 billion neuron computers that collectively produce seeing, hearing, feeling, thinking, planning, and doing.[317] Neurons do not work in isolation; their power is in their numbers.

When we have experiences, groups of neurons fire, making connections with others to form functional patterns relative to what we think and do. In his book *The Deep History of Ourselves*, Joseph LeDoux says that functions result from patterns formed by ensembles of neurons in one area that connect via output cables to ensembles in other areas, forming functional circuits.[318]

Our brain is a mass of computers and cables dynamically connecting through experience to form functional patterns that drive us. When hundreds to thousands of neurons send signals through circuits, we experience perception, movement, thought, and emotion.

To understand how a network can do anything, it helps to start with simple examples and work up from there. We often fail to notice, but networks are everywhere we look in human endeavors and nature. In modern society, humans use networks with the Internet, water systems, power grids, cell phones, artificial intelligence, and much more.

Nature is the originator, using networks everywhere in plant and animal life. The largest organism on earth is a 2.4-mile-wide honey fungus found in Oregon. With fungus, mushrooms grow on top of the soil, and a complex root system connects them underground. Nutrients flow through the root network, nourishing and sustaining all the connected mushrooms. Altogether, the honey fungus is a root network producing mushrooms over 2.4 miles, all of which represent one organism.

In the book *Elastic: Unlocking Your Brain's Ability to Embrace Change*, author Leonard Mlodinow looks at social insects like ants as an example of networks in animal life. Depending on the species, thousands to millions of ants live together in a colony, working as a collective unit. They form a society of nurses, architects, builders, scouts, hunters, gatherers, and many others who live to support the colony.[319]

Each ant is a single processing unit that sends and receives signals with others as they perform a job. If there is a danger, one ant can tell another, who will tell another, until the message reaches everyone in the colony. A single ant can trigger an evacuation message that the entire colony instantly responds to.

Every ant connects with others, who connect with others, and so on, until the whole colony is interconnected. Together, they form a complex network that integrates information from every ant into the colony, resulting in the emergent phenomenon of collective intelligence.[320]

When every ant communicates in a network, the colony takes on a singular identity. The colony is the combined processing power of all ants, sharing information, leading to collective intelligence that can evaluate situations and take meaningful action.[321] The colony can be considered a single organism that integrates information to make decisions.

Similarly, our brain is a colony of neurons that communicate collectively as a network to produce a singular identity. With its 86 billion neurons, the brain is almost 200 times the size of a typical ant colony.[322] Like ants, collective intelligence emerges when neurons integrate information as a complex network. Nature is all about networks, and ants are just the beginning.

Our first-person experience is the product of every neuron in a biological network communicating, as a single unit, to give rise to our collective intelligence. The brain is an integrated network of neurons that collectively have outstanding memory, storage, and speed.[323] It is a single large structure with distinct areas, each housing groups of neurons that vary in size, type, and configuration. The numbers and configuration of neurons can change in each area, but the general design is the same everywhere you look.

Computer-like neurons cram every millimeter of the brain's cellular space, and their output cables connect them all together. In each area, neurons are organized into layers that comprise thousands of neurons. These layers are arranged with the inputs to the neurons on one side and the outputs on the other. Multiple layers are then lined up one after the other, with the outputs of one layer facing the inputs of the next.

A neuron in one layer fires a chemical signal towards thousands of receiving neurons in the next. Some of those neurons will be triggered and fire, passing the signal to another layer to repeat the process. One activates others, who activate others, who do the same, forming a chain of connectivity from layer to layer. Each link in the chain connects neurons across layers, creating a cascading pattern of activity whenever one fires. A single neuron can connect to thousands of others, and these layered patterns contribute to circuits that transfer signals throughout the brain.

These are cascading waves of activity traveling through sheets of interconnected computer-like neurons that collectively integrate information, leading to thought and action. The brain is an extensive network of interlinked computers that form circuits with varying patterns of connectivity that continually fire to produce our reality. No part of the brain is isolated; every area is connected by circuits that integrate information through patterns.

We have a biological brain that wires patterns in real time based on what we do. It is a living network of neuron computers that connect through experience. When we are born, the brain has great potential: its structure and neurons are in place, but it has not yet had the opportunity to connect. Estimates show that, given all its potential connections, there are roughly 40 quadrillion possible patterns that can be etched into the brain.[324] We are born with some hardwired patterns, but it's experience that shapes the rest.

Our network and all its possible connections make up our potential. As we have experience, our network makes connections, forms patterns, and functional circuits emerge. When we repeat a thought or action, a similar pattern fires, connections adjust, and the signal is sent faster, tuning that circuit to send it more efficiently next time. By adulthood, a lifetime of thought and action wires specific connections, carving out patterns that shape how we think and act.

Every human brain is a network following a similar Homo sapiens design blueprint. There are billions of computers that form patterns based on what we do. These patterns are circuits that, when fired, create thoughts and actions. Each person's singular reality is the collective cellular effort of 86 billion neuron computers communicating as a network, and the 85 billion support cells that keep it working.

CHAPTER 19

Artificial Networks

Artificial intelligence has come a long way since its humble beginnings in the 1950s, with recent discoveries catapulting it into the mainstream.[325] The goal of the scientists and engineers behind it all has always been to build an intelligent machine equivalent to a human. Everything popping up in the field, from ChatGPT, self-driving cars, facial recognition, and smart assistants, stems from artificial networks inspired by the human brain.

These technologies use networks made of software or hardware nodes that represent simplified versions of neurons.[326] They mimic nature by combining artificial neurons with many connections into a network. Humans are only in the early stages of developing functional networks and are just beginning to realize their potential. Modern artificial networks are much simpler than their biological counterparts, but they serve as a good starting point for understanding how a network can lead to something substantial.

The current wave of AI, sparked by the works of Geoffrey Hinton and Ruslan Salakhutdinov in 2006, is powered by deep learning.[327] These networks place artificial nodes of varying numbers into single rows, called layers. The nodes in one layer are heavily connected to those in the next layer, forming rows of interconnected signaling units. Each layer processes information and passes the results to the next layer, gradually refining the solution. The last layer ties everything together to produce a result. Deep refers to the total number of layers in the network or how many layers deep it is.

Here is how it would work for a hypothetical six-layer photo-recognition network that can identify images of cats or dogs. The first layer of nodes is the input layer, which receives the signal and passes it through the network. The second layer analyzes pixel brightness, and the third identifies edges. The fourth layer detects textures, the fifth layer shapes, and the sixth layer ties it all together to provide an output answer.[328]

Generally, the first layer receives input and passes it to subsequent layers. These are called hidden layers, with each one solving a piece of the puzzle. They pass information in a pattern toward the final output layer, where it is combined. Information cascades from layer to layer, generating a collective response by the time it flows through the network. With our photo recognition network, an image of a cat or dog is fed as input, producing a specific pattern that allows the network to determine what it is by the time it reaches the output.

Modern AI, such as ChatGPT, self-driving vehicles, and image generators, consists of networks with different shapes, sizes, and configurations, comprising millions to billions of nodes arranged across hundreds of layers. They can do one thing well, usually better than any human, but that is all they can do. Our brain, on the other hand, has general intelligence, which means we can learn many things. Any person can learn to ride a bike, drive a car, and play an instrument. Both humans and AI use networks to function, but ours is far more complex and advanced.

To be fair, nature had a 3.8-billion-year head start in developing a biological network with general intelligence.[329] Humans have been at it for less than 100 years and are already building networks with billions of nodes, comparable in scale to a small mammal's brain, like a cat's, but far less complex.[330] We are seeing impressive results, but these are early representations of what a learning network can do.

Humans are nature's biological networks, now constructing their own artificial networks in an attempt to surpass themselves. Deep learning is only the beginning. Over time, more discoveries and breakthroughs may lead to networks with artificial general intelligence comparable to ours. However, there is a long way to go in size, connectivity, and structure before reaching that milestone.

CHAPTER 20

How Artificial Networks Learn

Modern technology owes itself to traditional rules-based computer programming.[331] Everything from Microsoft Word, Call of Duty, Minecraft, websites, apps, and social media relies on hardcoded step-by-step instructions to work.[332]

Coders write a series of commands, line after line, in a computer language, telling the program exactly what to do. Every program has thousands of lines of code that rigidly script out its behavior.[333] There are no surprises with this type of programming; the coder knows the outcome every time.

Behind AI is a flexible new approach in which the program is not given all the rules. Instead, the programmer sets up a network of artificial nodes organized in layers, providing it with a goal and a way to measure success. From there, data flows into the network and continually adjusts its connections, based on the information it receives. Rather than following prewritten instructions, the network shapes patterns through experience, creating its own rules.[334]

In 2015, the Google-backed startup DeepMind Technologies achieved a breakthrough by training a network to play the Atari game Breakout. It is like Brick Breaker, where a ball is hit into bricks with a paddle, and the game ends when the paddle misses the ball. The plan was to see if a network with a goal could learn by playing independently, rather than providing it with standard rules-based instructions telling it precisely what to do.

The DeepMind team gave the network the goal to maximize its points. The idea was to see whether it could learn from that instruction alone by adapting moves that lead to a high score. From there, they made it aware of the game screen and the current score so it could play the way we do. Finally, it started to play, and information from the game flowed through the network, adjusting its connections to reflect its learning.

When the DeepMind team turned the breakout playing network on for the first time, it did not know what it was doing. All of its moves were random, with it barely getting a score.[335] Gradually, the paddle began hitting the ball into the bricks, and the score went up. Every move that led to more points adjusted the network's connections, forming patterns it could use the next time it encountered a similar input. After playing hundreds of games, it learned through trial and error, molding patterns of responses that allowed it to play at an expert level.

Before playing Breakout, the DeepMind network was brand new. Its nodes were arranged in layers, but the connections between them were undefined, waiting to adjust through experience. As it played, data passed through the nodes of each layer, gradually adjusting those connections into distinct patterns to represent its learning.

The connections between nodes in the network continually strengthen and weaken as information passes through, forming specific patterns that achieve its goal. By exposing a network to vast amounts of data, it fails repeatedly, learning by trial and error.[336] Through mistakes, it tunes functional patterns that it uses to respond to similar scenarios in the future. It sounds simple, but after hundreds of games, the Breakout network played like an expert human player.

Networks differ from traditional rule-based programs. They are dynamic and continually adjust their connections in pursuit of an assigned objective. The programmer establishes the network but does not know what functional patterns will emerge to accomplish its goal.

Neural networks are more like children learning, and the programmer is the parent who trains them with data.[337] The networks behind self-driving vehicles have been trained by physically driving millions of miles and simulating billions more. It is a proven brute-force approach whereby continually feeding a network with data will eventually shape it into something functional.

AI and humans take a similar approach to learning, both leveraging networks that adjust through experience based on underlying goals and drives. In the brain, some circuits are hardwired through evolution, while others remain flexible and take shape through experience.

Our circuits that form through experience learn similarly to the breakout-playing artificial network discussed above, though they are far more complex. Neural networks must learn the hard way by bumping into things and making mistakes. The nature of a network, whether artificial or biological, is to adjust through experience, shaping a framework of understanding around its innate goal. The human network is more sophisticated in design, but the takeaway is that a network with a goal and a way to measure success can learn.

CHAPTER 21

Human Networks

Neural networks first appeared in simple, jellyfish-like creatures over 600 million years ago and have been evolving in complexity across different worm, insect, fish, amphibian, reptile, bird, and mammal species ever since.[338] Each of these animal categories can be thought of as a distinct class of networks, marking significant advances in neural design. Nature has produced millions to billions of species within each class, all with networks unique to that design. The network is modified and configured differently for each species, as nature trials networks through countless living prototypes.

Nature is like an AI company that manufactures smart robots with networks. The company would start by producing small, simple robots that improve in functionality with each new model, until it arrives at a design with human intelligence. Nearly every animal that has ever come into existence is a living robot, a product of a different make and model, with a unique network that drives it. After hundreds of millions of years and trialing countless animal robot products, nature put the Homo sapiens model into production about 200,000 years ago.[339]

Imagine a company that successfully creates an artificially intelligent humanoid robot equivalent to us. They would be mass-produced according to the Homo sapiens 2.0 blueprint, all coming out of the box equipped with a network of the same general design. Similarly, humans are nature's mass-produced, biologically intelligent products, with networks that follow the same Homo sapiens specification.

From the moment we're conceived, our genes get to work constructing us from one cell, according to the human genetic blueprint.[340] We are all biological Homo sapiens robot products fitted with a brain of that design. The brain bubbles up from the spine and forms a structure divided and subdivided into specialized regions, each populated with cells.[341] After we are born, the brain continues to grow, reaching 90 percent of its adult size by age 6, spending another 20-30 years wiring itself to maturity.[342]

Our genes are like AI programmers who build a learning network that takes shape from the information it receives. Genes hardwire some patterns into our network as they download reflexive survival behaviors that worked for earlier versions of us.[343] A baby's ability to take to the breast is a functional neural pattern pre-wired into the brain.[344] These are fundamental functional circuits, installed by our genes, that provide the base survival programs for when we are born and throughout our lives. Outside these prewired behaviors lie hundreds of trillions of possible connections between neurons that wire with less genetic restraint.[345]

The approach is simple: overpopulate the brain with neurons that must fire signals or die. From as early as conception, information from the environment is received, activating some neurons while others remain dormant. Our brain operates on the principle of survival of the busiest: neurons that fire become part of circuits and live, while those that do not wither away and die.[346] At the same time, support cells nourish active neurons and add myelin to output cables that fire most often.

Our network continually adjusts as we interact with our environment through a fundamental process called plasticity. Neurons that fire form connections and create patterns that become part of the circuits that drive us, while those that do not fire prune away and die as our experience molds how we think and feel.

In 1949, Canadian Psychologist Donald Hebb captured the essence of plasticity with the principle, neurons that fire together wire together, known as Hebb's law.[347] It works the same way as artificial networks that continually refine connections through experience, but in the brain, we call that process plasticity.

When we are born, much of the brain is pure potential. Our genes set up the network, putting our neurons into position, while many of the connections between them are left undefined. When we have an experience, specific neurons fire, creating a cascading wave of activity in which particular connections are selected, and a corresponding pattern emerges.

With repetition, we fire and wire distinct patterns that represent our habits, actions, behaviors, and thoughts.[348] Genes build the network, but it is plasticity that uses information from our environment to define which connections to use, shaping who we are emotionally, mentally, and physically.[349]

Even our eyesight, which we assume comes automatically from genes, is shaped by plasticity. Genes connect our eyes to the rest of the brain, establishing the wiring to see, but they do not know what they will see. From the moment we are born, information flows through our eyes, forming the patterns that shape how we see the world in a period of critical plasticity.[350]

Suppose a baby is born with cataracts or a cloudy deposit in one or both eyes that are not removed within the first few weeks of life. In adulthood, they would have impairments in seeing fine visual details, recognizing faces, and detecting specific complex movements.[351] However, if doctors remove the cataracts early, the baby will have normal vision as an adult. Our experience helps shape everything from our most basic senses to our most complex behaviors and actions.[352]

Every person enters the world with a learning network of activity-dependent neurons that form patterns through experience via plasticity. From birth through childhood, the brain is most plastic as it grows and forms the patterns that will drive us as adults.[353] It is an impersonal process in which the environment molds the brain, shaping who we are. The brain does not ask questions; it unbiasedly makes connections. The brain does not consider whether something is right or wrong; it simply wires what we think and do most often.[354]

By adulthood, we have spent a lifetime unknowingly wiring our network to maturity, forming the model for how we will see the world. Fortunately, the brain never loses its plasticity; it remains malleable throughout our lives. While brain plasticity is most significant in childhood, it continues across our lifespan, allowing us to rewire patterns and behaviors at any age.

Before I was thirty, I knew nothing about the contents within this book. After over ten years of effort, listening to audiobooks, writing, researching, and applying it to my life for thousands of hours, I have wired the knowledge into my brain.

If we are asleep at the wheel and align with all of our self-driving decisions, our wiring remains essentially unchanged. At any time in our lives, we can wake up our driver to take control, using attention to leverage the impartial power of plasticity and shape our brains in the direction we want.

CHAPTER 22

How Human Networks Learn

Our brain is a learning network that uses plasticity to form circuits that become the automatic thoughts, behaviors, habits, skills, and actions that drive us.[355] Outside of hardwired patterns are those that take shape through experience. There are billions of neurons whose connections remain activity-dependent and adjust according to what we do most. From birth on, everything we sense, feel, and think produces a corresponding wave of activity that becomes a pattern physically embedded in our brain.[356]

To understand learning through plasticity, it is best to explore what happens in the brain when we first learn how to ride a bike. We cannot just jump on and ride, because a pattern for that function does not yet exist. It is not personal; we just can't perform a function without first tuning a pattern for it. Many of our thoughts, habits, actions, behaviors, and skills are patterns tuned from scratch until they become automatic functions.

When riding a bike for the first time, we pedal, moving the handlebars back and forth as we try to balance, only to inevitably fall. During that initial experience, specific neurons fire and wire together, creating a corresponding pattern for riding the bike. We fall because we have yet to establish a pattern for that function.

On the second try, a similar pattern fires again, but any changes to our approach cause the neurons to fire slightly differently, altering the pattern. External adjustments have corresponding internal effects that activate particular neurons. These changes trigger new neurons that join the pattern, while others that were previously used may no longer fire and be excluded. At the same time, the synaptic connections between neurons continually strengthen and weaken, while continued activation may draw the attention of our broadband installers, who add myelin. All of these factors work together to refine the pattern and send signals more efficiently.

The bike riding pattern fires again and again, each time we ride, continuously refining until we can do it without falling. Eventually, with enough attempts, we tune a functional pattern that sends signals at the right speed and time, making riding the bike an automatic function. Once learned, we can select and fire that pattern at any time, performing that function without a second thought.

As with riding a bike, every thought, habit, action, behavior, or skill we learn follows the same impersonal process of refining patterns through repetition until they become automatic.[357] Learning is the result of neurons and support cells continually tuning patterns for the thoughts and actions we repeatedly engage in.[358] Eventually, the signal flows through the pattern at the right speed and time, reaching a tipping point where it becomes an automatic function.[359]

We have roughly 600 trillion connections in the brain, many of which are flexible and ready to form patterns based on what we think and do most often.[360] Everything we learn is plasticity, impartially firing and wiring patterns based on repetition until they become automatic.[361] A lifetime of experience wires a storehouse of automated functions that our self-driving system or driver can use at a moment's notice.

The brain is all about automating what we do most. Performing a function for the first time takes full attention. Each time we do it, the pattern fires and tunes a little more, sending signals faster.[362] With enough repetition, it becomes an automatic function we can perform with minimal attention.[363]

Automating what we do most has several advantages. Without automation, each task would have to be approached as if we were encountering it for the first time.[364] Imagine how frustrating it would be if, after the tenth time riding the bike, we weren't any better than on the first try.

Another benefit of automating functions is that we can do them without thinking, freeing our driver to focus on more pressing matters. Automation allowed our ancestors to walk without thinking while focusing on potential prey when hunting.[365] Through experience, we unknowingly fill our brains with patterns of thought and movement that we can automatically perform with minimal awareness.[366]

The other side of learning is unlearning. We learned to ride a bike by taking action, firing and wiring the pattern to support it. If we suddenly stop riding the bike forever, we stop firing that pattern altogether. Since our neurons must stay active to survive, they repurpose themselves by pruning and growing connections to join other patterns, in an attempt to remain relevant. That is another characteristic of plasticity known as "neurons that fire apart wire apart," or "if you don't use it, you lose it."[367]

Depending on what we learn, some traces of the pattern may remain even years after we stop doing it, but our proficiency still declines. At a cellular level, when we do something, a pattern forms and we learn; if we stop, the pattern repurposes itself, and we unlearn.

We unintentionally spend our childhoods through our mid-twenties wiring our experiences into a network that, in adulthood, emerges as the automatic, self-driving responses that drive us. Plasticity shapes who we are and how we see the world, automating what we do most. There is no right or wrong to the brain; if we do something enough, it becomes an automatic thought, behavior, habit, action, or skill, no questions asked.

Fortunately, the brain remains plastic throughout our lives; who we are is not fixed, and we can use our driver to change it into anything we want at any time. Many people do not change because they continue repeating the same self-driving patterns day in and day out, only strengthening and automating those responses further. If we are asleep at the wheel and let automatic self-driving decisions go unchecked, they remain unchanged.

To change, we must engage our driver with deliberate attention, repeating the thoughts and actions we want until they become our new automatic responses. At the same time, we have to interrupt our self-driving response and stop doing what we don't like so that we can unwire those undesirable automated patterns. By deliberately choosing the thoughts and actions we want and avoiding those we don't, especially with practices like mindfulness, our driver can harness the power of plasticity to rewire our brains toward whatever we desire.

CHAPTER 23

Tuning Mastery

We are human vehicles equipped with a learning network that impartially wires experiences into functional patterns that represent our skills and abilities. When we are born, our genes hardwire survival patterns, like recoiling from pain and feeding—the rest of the skills we acquire come from interacting with our environment. Our ability to walk, talk, read, and play a sport or an instrument is a pattern wired through repetition until it becomes an automatic function.[368]

The brain is an impartial learning network that tunes what we do the most into functional patterns, no questions asked. Generally, the more time we spend performing a skill, the better we become. With a skill like driving, it takes about 50 hours of practice to learn how to drive a car at a basic level, and another 10,000 hours of deliberate practice to be an expert race-car driver.[369]

The magic number for tuning a skill pattern to a master level is roughly 10,000 hours of effort.[370] Every brain has the potential to achieve mastery in any skill we choose. Studies of expert violinists, chess players, writers, figure skaters, and doctors reveal that 10,000 hours is typically required to tune our network to an expert level in any domain.[371]

Florida State University psychologist K. Anders Ericsson's research on expertise popularized and validated the 10,000-hour rule.[372] In the early 1990s, he and colleagues conducted a study with violinists at Berlin's elite Academy of Music to determine why some violinists are better than others.[373] The professors helped divide the students into three groups based on their skill levels. The first group was the stars likely to become world-class performers. The second group was highly capable, and the third group was expected to become music teachers.[374]

Throughout the study, students kept a detailed log of their weekly practice hours.[375] The research team then determined how much of that practice time was spent going through the motions on autopilot versus using deliberate, effortful attention to improve specific aspects of the skill. They found that the first two groups spent about 50-60 hours per week playing the violin, with 25 of those hours in deliberate, solitary practice.[376] The elite performers were spending at least four hours a day in targeted effortful practice.[377]

The difference between violin players was even more noticeable when the students tallied total practice hours over their lifetime. By age eighteen, the first group had accumulated 7,410 hours, the second 5,301 hours, and the third 3,420.[378] By the time the first group turned twenty, they had amassed roughly 10,000 hours of practice.[379] Simply playing for 10,000 hours does not make an expert; it takes focused, deliberate practice, attending to every detail, to reach master-level status.

When we learn a skill for the first time, like riding a bike, we fully engage in the activity, giving it our full driver's attention. Eventually, after falling off several times and taking corrective action, we tune a pattern that lets us ride the bike on autopilot without thinking. Automating a skill requires making mistakes with full attention until the pattern is tuned to the point where it becomes an automatic function that can be performed with little conscious effort. Once we learn to ride a bike, it is easy; we just hop on and ride down the street using minimal attention.

When we perform a skill automatically, we select and fire the pattern we wired through attention. Attention tunes patterns; autopilot uses them. When we execute a skill on autopilot with minimal attention, improvement is negligible because it takes full attention to tune patterns.[380]

When we ride a bike without thinking, we are merely selecting and firing the stored pattern that leads to that function. It is executing the pattern, not tuning it, so our skill level stays the same. Even if we rode for 10,000 hours on autopilot, we still wouldn't be that proficient. If we automate a skill, then only perform it on autopilot, we will see minimal improvement, no matter how much time we spend on it. We must continually refine our patterns with attention, as when first learning, to improve our skill level in any domain on the road to mastery.

We can do that by pushing to the edge of our ability and intentionally focusing on improving every movement and facet of that skill. If, after learning to ride the bike, we decide we want to jump a curb, that function requires a pattern. We must ride into the curb and fall over many times until we automate that ability. Jumping a curb, popping a wheelie, and riding with no hands are all sub-skill patterns related to the larger bike-riding pattern, and all must be tuned through attention if we want to be proficient at that skill overall.

Ericsson and colleagues determined that to reach mastery, we have to tune every subset of a skill with deliberate practice.[381] It is a specialized practice focused on placing our full scope of attention on specific movements in our game, yet to be perfected.[382] To improve at any skill, all we have to do is identify individual elements of our performance that need improvement and deliberately practice them with full driver attention.[383]

Remember, attention is a spotlight cued by both the self-driving system and our driver that forms patterns, turning whatever it repeatedly shines on into automatic functions. When we are born, we have minimal control over the spotlight, but as our driver develops, we can choose what it shines on and form the patterns we want. If we automate a function and run it on autopilot, our attention is not fully engaged, so improvement is minimal. To wire a skill to mastery, we have to keep tuning the pattern by continually shining the spotlight through deliberate practice. After 10,000 hours of continuous, focused tuning, anyone can become an expert in any domain.

Those who attain mastery are constantly fighting the urge to perform on autopilot by continually attending to what they can't do until it becomes automatic.[384] Deliberate practice is not fun; it requires us to consistently attend to our weaknesses in full driver attention, which is frustrating, tiring, and overwhelming.

It is natural to avoid struggle because it is hard, but that is when new connections form and the pattern adjusts.[385] It is essential to identify areas of weakness and make mistakes so we can tune those patterns into strengths. Most of us avoid the discomfort of making mistakes and get upset when we do. Placing our driver's spotlight of attention toward areas of weakness in deliberate practice refines the patterns further, improving our skill and making us better when we perform on autopilot.

To attain mastery, we must change our perspective on mistakes because they are the guideposts to expertise.[386] Reaching to the edge of our ability, failing, and reaching again is the only way to achieve mastery.[387] When we fail and course-correct, the brain adjusts the pattern, leading to greater skill. For mastery, we need to make every possible mistake to tune a pattern that can do it automatically, free of mistakes.[388] Mistakes are the best thing we can do on the path to greatness; they lead to growth and should be celebrated.

Mastery is available to anyone willing to get on the path and stay on it. We must look foolish and persevere through the instinct to stop. Mastery is an impersonal, universal process that our driver can wire into our brain with 10,000 hours of deliberate practice. It is simple in theory but difficult in practice, making expertise seem unattainable for most.

The most significant human achievers, such as Thomas Edison, Albert Einstein, Michael Jordan, Marie Curie, and many others, were overlooked when they were young.[389] They were not born into greatness; they worked tirelessly in the background, using deliberate practice to tune patterns to that level. They did not come into the world as unique; what made them special was that they got on the path and never got off, tuning patterns that achieved extraordinary results. If anything, the most elite humans have exceptional executive control, as they have spent thousands of hours at the wheel, deliberately tuning the networks that led to their accomplishments.

Even Mozart was not born predestined for greatness; his success resulted from more than 10,000 hours of deliberate practice. From the age of three, he played the piano obsessively.[390] His father, Leopold, was an accomplished musician, composer, and teacher who poured all his energy into making Mozart and his sister master musicians.[391]

Mozart worked tirelessly, and his father helped him use deliberate practice to tune master patterns. Although he composed for a decade by age fifteen, experts consider those works curiosities. He was not considered a world-class composer until adolescence.[392] Mozart was not born with the pattern for what he did; he refined it through deliberate practice from the age of three under the guidance of an expert.

Tiger Woods and the Williams sisters are other examples of those who spent their early years practicing more than 10,000 hours under the tutelage of their parents. These individuals were not born into greatness; they spent their lives tirelessly engaging driver attention in deliberate practice as they strategically tuned the patterns that led to world-class results.

We often attribute the accomplishments of the most successful performers to talent, saying they were just born that way. However, talent is what we have before we start, and skill is what we acquire through continually engaging attention in deliberate practice, regardless of talent. Some are born with a genetic head start, but they still have to tune that pattern to mastery. Not even the most talented person can achieve mastery without spending thousands of hours deliberately tuning the skill with attention.[393] There is no shortcut to mastery, regardless of how much talent we start with. We are not born with master patterns prewired in our network; they must be tuned through deliberate attention, no matter who we are; there is no way around it.

Nothing will happen if we are born with a talent but fail to refine it through deliberate practice with driver attention. On the other hand, if we are not born with talent but put in 10,000 hours of focused effort, mastery is still within reach.[394] If our view on talent prevents us from putting in the work, then why have it?

It is best to depersonalize mastery as a process, get on the path, and see what happens. People are not born into greatness, nor are they restricted from attaining it.[395] Every healthy brain is a learning network with the same potential to tune to mastery, regardless of age, sex, class, or race. Mastery is not reserved for the super-talented; anyone can reach it with at least 10,000 hours of deliberate practice.[396] Reaching mastery is using driver attention to take the wheel from our self-driving system over and over, continuously engaging in deliberate practice until we tune a pattern that leads to extraordinary results.

In reality, we are lucky if it only takes 10,000 hours to achieve mastery. Ed Catmull, co-founder of Pixar, spent twenty years working toward the singular goal of making Toy Story.[397] The computer animation technology for the movie did not exist; he had to invent it over decades of deliberate effort that never quit.

Author Napoleon Hill spent 25 years crafting his book *Think and Grow Rich.*[398] To reach mastery, we must change our attitudes toward achieving our goals. There is no shortcut or quick fix to tune the brain to mastery; it cannot happen overnight.[399] It is a slow process available to anyone willing to get on the path and stay on it.

While writing this book, my self-driving system generated thousands of self-deprecating thoughts. It would say, "Who do you think you are? You are nobody. No one will read your book. Just stop." I ignored those thoughts, reminding myself that success is a process, and kept taking the wheel with my driver to write. I wrote for 20-30 hours a week for over six years, depersonalizing the process, and slowly but surely, the book came together.

Ten thousand hours of deliberate practice don't guarantee we'll become the LeBron James of our domain.[400] We likely won't be the best in the world, but we will have a pattern capable of performing at an expert level. At forty years old, no amount of practice would get me into the NBA; it is impossible. Even if I started practicing at 4 years old and put in the required hours, I might still not make it into the NBA. I could play basketball at an expert level, but I may not be among the best in the world. The only guarantee on the road to mastery is that, without continually engaging attention through deliberate practice, it is impossible to become the best.

Whoever we may be, we have a learning network that takes at least 10,000 hours of tuning to reach mastery in any domain. It is never too late; we can take the wheel with deliberate attention and start tuning any pattern of our choice to mastery at any age. Of course, it is best to begin in childhood, when the brain is most plastic, and we have time.

It becomes more challenging as adults, due to added responsibilities and limited time for practice. Still, Charles Darwin didn't release *On the Origin of Species* until he was fifty. Vera Wang entered the fashion world at forty, and Julia Child wrote her first cookbook when she was fifty. It is never too late to get on the path and use our driver to take full advantage of our neural network's potential. We put more limits on ourselves than our brains ever will. We all have an impartial learning network that we can tune to a master level with our driver at any age, regardless of who we are. Just start engaging the driver's full attention in deliberate practice and don't stop until mastery is achieved.

CHAPTER 24

Mental Practice

Imagine eating a sour candy, hearing the sound of nails on a chalkboard, jumping into a freezing shower, thinking of an enemy, sunbathing at the beach, or performing in front of a crowd. Simply thinking of sights, sounds, smells, tactile sensations, or emotional events can trigger a whole-body response in the same way as the real thing.

Brain scans using fMRI demonstrate that many of the same neurons and regions of the brain become activated whether we're imagining an event or actually living it.[401] The brain does not know the difference between thinking and doing; both activate similar patterns of neurons.[402]

When we tune networks to mastery with our driver through deliberate practice, we automatically assume we are talking about physical training. However, many studies now show that observing others and visualizing an activity are also practical approaches to tuning skills to a master level.[403] A survey of US Olympians shows that 90 percent of athletes and 94 percent of coaches use mental imagery as part of their training regimen for competition.[404]

Most of us unknowingly use the power of imagery all day long, replaying past and future scenarios in our minds. Mental training involves deliberately using the power of thought to visualize ourselves physically performing a skill, which activates relevant neurons, refines the pattern, and increases our proficiency.

In the book *Neurologic*, Eliezer Sternberg discusses a study by Dr. Guang Yue of the Cleveland Clinic, in which participants exercised their elbows and pinkies. Participants were split into three practice groups: physical, mental, and control, with the control group doing nothing. The first two groups spent 15 minutes daily, 5 days a week, flexing their pinky and elbow over 12 weeks. The group that physically practiced showed a 50% improvement in muscle strength. Surprisingly, the mental training group that only visualized the activity also showed gains in muscle strength, with increases of 13.5% in the elbow and 35% in the pinky.[405] There were no improvements in the control group, as expected.

Dr. Yue concluded that mentally practicing a motor event triggers neurons to fire in a pattern similar to that during physical execution, resulting in improved performance.[406] The mental practice group showed less improvement than the physical practice group, but this still shows that mental training has a positive effect. Visualizing ourselves performing a skill activates neurons in that pattern, tunes it more, and leads to increased ability.

The book *The Leading Brain* shares findings from similar research inspired by Yue's work, showing that those who visualized exercising increased their strength by about 22 percent, compared with 30 percent for those who trained physically.[407] By vividly picturing ourselves performing an activity, we fire neurons in that pattern and tune them further. We are not saying we can get by on mental rehearsal alone, or that it's as effective as physical practice. Mental practice is a valuable tool that complements physical training and should be a part of our toolkit when tuning a skill to an expert level.[408]

Visualizing ourselves performing a skill in the virtual arena of our mind is a mental practice that the most elite athletes use to help tune their patterns and achieve mastery.[409] All it takes is vividly picturing ourselves performing in real time as though it were happening, imagining the sights, sounds, smells, sensations, and feelings as we successfully execute the skill.[410]

The more realistic we can make the scene in our mind, the greater the tuning for that skill.[411] It is a mental arena where we can safely make and learn from mistakes. Through this mental rehearsal, we can refine the pattern and improve, all in the comfort of our minds.

A basketball player may visualize the final seconds of a game in which their team is down by 1 point and they have the ball. They picture the basketball court, with players on the floor and fans eagerly watching from the stands. They feel their firm grip on the ball as they steadily dribble up and down, waiting for the right opportunity to shoot.

They visualize themselves stepping toward a defender, pushing off, and shooting the perfect fadeaway shot. They feel the ball leave their fingers and watch as it soars toward the basket with the buzzer sounding midair. The ball hits the rim and spins around before finally dropping in. At that moment, everyone celebrates as they make the winning shot.

The more we see ourselves successfully navigating these high-pressure scenarios, the more prepared we will be during the actual event. If we have mentally rehearsed a scenario a hundred times, we will be ready, with a pattern in place, when we encounter the real thing. Mental rehearsal allows us to tune patterns for experiences we have yet to encounter.

Michael Jordan was known for saying that he took more shots in his mind than ever on the court.[412] We have nothing to lose with mental practice, as it is all in the comfort of our minds. We can improve a skill with as few as two to three 15-minute weekly sessions.[413]

Mental practice may be challenging at first if we are not used to it, but, as with anything, the more we practice, the better we get. Visualizing ourselves performing a skill is especially difficult if we have limited experience in that domain. If we have never played basketball, creating a vivid mental picture will be challenging, but if we have played for thousands of hours, we can produce a crystal-clear mental image.[414]

By now, it is clear that thinking and doing are not too different in the cellular space of our brain, as both fire similar patterns. A lifetime of unknowingly automating patterns based on what we think and do the most determines the self-driving functions that drive us. At any time, we can deliberately engage driver attention with the physical or mental events of our choosing to weave any pattern we desire. Deliberate attention is the driver's secret power for mastering any skill, behavior, habit, or action we choose. The brain only knows to automate what we pay attention to; no questions asked. We just have to take the wheel with our driver, and our network will obediently follow, regardless of who we are.

CHAPTER 25

Genetic Potential

If nature is an AI company manufacturing different products with networks, then genes are what build them. Genes construct each of us from a single cell, according to our Homo sapiens blueprint. Some believe that who we are is rigid and predetermined by our genes. The reality is that who we become is not set in stone, and our potential is far more flexible than we could ever imagine.

The latest discoveries in genetics, neuroscience, and psychology show that the environment plays a significant role in gene expression.[415] The old idea of "nature versus nurture" is now outdated as a model for explaining how we develop into who we are.[416] *We are neither born nor made. The environment is inseparable from our genes*.[417] The new way of looking at genes is gene-environment interaction (GxE).[418] Genes are not fixed; they do not follow a predefined script; they continually shift and adapt to an ever-changing environment.

In his book *The Genius in All of Us*, David Shenk explains genes as roughly more than 20,000-volume knobs and switches that the environment continually adjusts.[419] Each gene has tiny epigenetic markers along its surface that receive chemical signals from the environment, enabling the external world to interact with and influence gene behavior.[420] These marks make the environment the hands that turn our genetic knobs and switches. Epigenetics sees genes and the environment as inseparable and symbiotic; we cannot have one without the other.[421]

When we come into the world, genes provide us with a switchboard full of knobs and switches. Initially, genes preset our knobs at specific levels and place our switches in on or off positions. These initial settings set the stage for our physical, intellectual, and personality traits.[422]

Some of the knobs and switches for traits like height are more rigidly defined, and the environment exerts less influence on them. Others, such as personality and temperament, are more flexible, and the environment constantly adjusts them, turning them up or down, on or off.[423] Genes initially set the knobs and switches to give me brown hair, but environmental factors like sunlight, stress, and chemicals adjust them to change their color. Even if we are predisposed to certain traits, the environment still influences their development.

The environment is a complex force that continuously manipulates our knobs and switches from conception onward, refining the traits we start with. Internally, we have hormones, metabolism, various cell types, different developmental stages, and thoughts. Externally, we have diet, physical activity, social interactions, stressors, toxins, temperature, and light.[424] Throughout our lives, these internal and external environmental factors act as the hands that turn our knobs and switches, shaping how we take form.

Having a gene does not determine who we become; it must be turned on or expressed.[425] Some genes can remain dormant forever, waiting for the environment to trigger them.[426] Just because we have a knob or switch does not mean it will be on or set to the max.

Interactions with the environment continually express our genes and influence their position. Genes matter, but they do not determine physical and character traits on their own.[427] Environmental forces impact the expression of our genes. We may be born with certain traits, but environmental factors help influence how they are expressed, shaping who we are.

A comprehensive analysis of nearly 3,000 studies involving 14.6 million twins found that heritability across all traits is about 49%.[428] That is a generalized average across all traits, as genes determine up to 90 percent of some, and only 20 percent of others. The environment adjusts them the rest of the way, impacting some traits more than others.

Knobs and switches for physical characteristics tend to be more fixed in position, whereas intelligence, personality, and temperament are more responsive to environmental factors. We come with some genetic constraints, but there's no saying how far the environment can take them. Although genes establish our volume knobs and switches, the environment significantly influences their expression.

Every experience we have turns some knobs and not others. Getting into a fight, studying, practicing skills, or watching TV are all different environmental factors that produce unique imprints on our genes. Our genes do not ask questions; they obediently adjust according to the environment we are in, regardless of whether it is good or bad for us.[429] The environments we spend the most time in alter our knobs and switches, helping influence who we become. We spend our whole lives unknowingly allowing our environment to dictate how our genes are expressed.

If our self-driving system is the primary driver performing 80-95 percent of the driving, it is the one responding to these environments, influencing how our genes express from moment to moment. Our survival, intuitive, and default mode circuits continually make decisions based on our environment, and our genes obediently respond accordingly. If we never challenge our self-driving system, its automatic responses to our environment will be the primary shaper of our genetic expression.

However, at any time, we can strategically use our environment to shape our genes in the direction we choose. Consciously using our driver to select the environments we expose ourselves to allows us to take control of our genetic switchboard. A professional athlete, actor, musician, or monk spends thousands of hours practicing in a particular environment. Every second spent in training adjusts their genetic knobs and switches toward their skill.

Genes respond adaptively to our environment, so directing how we spend our time with our driver gives us a say in how we develop. If our self-driving system chronically triggers stressful acceleration, it will express our genes in a more harmful way.

However, if we use our driver to interrupt that response by mindfully turning to our breath and applying the brake, we can express our genes more beneficially.

We are not born predestined to any life; by dictating how we spend our time, we take our destiny into our own hands. With gene-environment interaction, we can unlock the potential of our genes in any domain we choose. We put far more limitations on ourselves than our genes ever will.

When trying to attain self or professional mastery, do not think about genes. Simply get on the path and expose yourself to environments aligned with your goals, and our genes will obey. We will only know our true genetic potential after spending thousands of hours deliberately expressing our genes with our driver. If we remain asleep at the wheel, our self-driving system will continue to dictate our lives. It is time to take the wheel with your driver to intervene with our self-driving system and unlock our potential. With deliberate attention, our driver can direct our vehicle in any direction we choose, and the brain and body will follow. Just take the wheel and don't stop until you get there.

Endnotes

Chapter 1

1. Vivek Wadhwa and Alex Salkever, *The Driver in the Driverless Car: How Your Technology Choices Create the Future* (Berrett-Koehler Publishers, 2019), p. 149.
2. Michael Wooldridge, *A Brief History of Artificial Intelligence: What It Is, Where We Are, and Where We Are Going* (Flatiron Books, 2021), p. 176.
3. Lawrence D. Burns and Christopher Shulgan, *Autonomy: The Quest to Build the Driverless Car—and How It Will Reshape Our World* (Ecco, 2018), p. 224.
4. Janelle Shane, *You Look Like a Thing, and I Love You: How Artificial Intelligence Works and Why It's Making the World a Weirder Place* (Voracious, 2019), p. 55.
5. Wadhwa and Salkever, *Driver in the Driverless Car*, p. 106.
6. Luke Dormehl, *Thinking Machines: The Quest for Artificial Intelligence—and Where It's Taking Us Next* (TarcherPerigee, 2017), p. 172.
7. Burns and Shulgan, *Autonomy*, p. 224.
8. Marcus du Sautoy, *The Creativity Code: Art and Innovation in the Age of AI* (Belknap Press, 2019), p. 84.
9. Shane, *You Look Like a Thing*, p. 9.
10. Shane, *You Look Like a Thing*, p. 115.
11. Daniel Goleman, *Focus: The Hidden Driver of Excellence* (Harper, 2013), p. 164.
12. Du Sautoy, *Creativity Code*, p. 18
13. Jeff Hawkins, *A Thousand Brains: A New Theory of Intelligence* (Basic Books, 2021), p. 182.
14. Wooldridge, *Brief History of Artificial Intelligence*, p. 149.

15. Shane, *You Look Like a Thing*, p. 59.
Wooldridge, *Brief History of Artificial Intelligence*, p. 155.
16. Shane, *You Look Like a Thing*, p. 59.
17. Shane, *You Look Like a Thing*, p. 59.
18. Shane, *You Look Like a Thing*, p. 20.
19. Shane, *You Look Like a Thing*, p. 59.
20. Wooldridge, *Brief History of Artificial Intelligence*, p. 155.
21. Shane, *You Look Like a Thing*, p. 57.
22. Eric Topol, *Deep Medicine: How Artificial Intelligence Can Make Healthcare Human Again* (Basic Books, 2019), p. 87.
23. Wooldridge, *Brief History of Artificial Intelligence*, p. 153.
24. Wooldridge, *Brief History of Artificial Intelligence*, p. 154.

Chapter 2

25. Jonathan Haidt, *The Happiness Hypothesis: Finding Modern Truth in Ancient Wisdom* (Basic Books, 2006), p. 15.
26. Haidt, *Happiness Hypothesis*, p. 15.
27. Chip Heath and Dan Heath, *Switch: How to Change Things When Change Is Hard* (Random House Canada, 2010), p. 6.
28. Daniel G. Amen and Tana Amen, *The Brain Warrior's Way*, p. 213.
29. Haidt, *Happiness Hypothesis*, p. 29.
30. David G. Myers, *How Do We Know Ourselves? Curiosities and Marvels of the Human Mind* (Farrar, Straus and Giroux, 2022), p. 26.

Chapter 3

31. Lee Pulos, *Beyond Hypnosis* (Ascent Audio, 2015), p. 110.
32. Leonard Mlodinow, *Subliminal: How Your Unconscious Mind Rules Your Behavior* (Vintage, 2012), p. 33.
33. John Yates et al., *The Mind Illuminated: A Complete Meditation Guide Integrating Buddhist Wisdom and Brain Science for Greater Mindfulness* (Atria Books, 2017), p. 345.
34. Mariano Sigman, *The Secret Life of the Mind: How Your Brain Thinks, Feels, and Decides* (Little, Brown Spark, 2017), p. 104.
35. Bruce H. Lipton, *The Biology of Belief: 10th Anniversary Edition* (Hay House, 2015), p. 174
36. Friederike Fabritius and Hans W. Hagemann, *The Leading Brain* (TarcherPerigee, 2017), p. 148.

37.Fabritius and Hagemann, *Leading Brain*, p. 143.
38.Joseph LeDoux, *Synaptic Self: How Our Brains Become Who We Are* (Penguin Books, 2003), p. 10.
39.Joseph LeDoux, *Anxious: Using the Brain to Understand and Treat Fear and Anxiety* (Penguin Books, 2015), p. 1.
40.LeDoux, *Anxious*, p. 148.
41.Eliezer Sternberg, *Neurologic: The Brain's Hidden Rationale Behind Our Irrational Behavior* (Vintage, 2016), p. 8.
42.Sigman, *Secret Life of the Mind*, p. 104.
43.Stephen L. Macknik et al., *Sleights of Mind* (Henry Holt and Co., 2024), p.181.
44.Mlodinow, *Subliminal*, p. 33.
45.Myers, *How Do We Know Ourselves?*, p. 26.
46.Gary John Bishop, *Unfu*k Yourself: Get Out of Your Head and into Your Life (HarperOne, 2017), p. 58.

Chapter 4

47.Peter C. Whybrow, *The Well-Tuned Brain: The Remedy for a Manic Society* (W. W. Norton, 2015), p. 58.
48.Dean Buonomano, *Brain Bugs: How the Brain's Flaws Shape Our Lives* (W. W. Norton, 2011), p. 161.
49.Sam Harris, *Waking Up: A Guide to Spirituality Without Religion* (Simon & Schuster, 2014), p. 75.
50.Buonomano, *Brain Bugs*, p. 169.
51.Daniel Kahneman, *Thinking, Fast and Slow* (Doubleday Canada, 2011), p. 323.
52.Kahneman, *Thinking, Fast and Slow*, p. 95.
53.Buonomano, *Brain Bugs*, p. 169.
54.Whybrow, *Well-Tuned Brain*, p. 58.
55.Buonomano, *Brain Bugs*, p. 169.
56.Buonomano, *Brain Bugs*, p. 161.
57.Judson Brewer, *The Craving Mind* (Yale University Press, 2017), p. 86.
58.Brewer, *Craving Mind*, p. 86.
59.Whybrow, *Well-Tuned Brain*, p. 7.
60.Kahneman, *Thinking, Fast and Slow*, p. 27/415.
61.Brewer, *Craving Mind*, p. 87.
62.LeDoux, *Anxious*, p. 81.

63.Kahneman, *Thinking, Fast and Slow*, p. 20.
64.Kahneman, *Thinking, Fast and Slow*, p. 24.
65.Harris, *Waking Up*, p. 75.
66.Kahneman, *Thinking, Fast and Slow*, p. 24.
67.Kahneman, *Thinking, Fast and Slow*, p. 24.

Chapter 5

68.Shane, *You Look Like a Thing*, p. 22.
69.Shane, *You Look Like a Thing*, p. 9.
70.John Brockman, ed., *What to Think About Machines That Think: Today's Leading Thinkers on the Age of Machine Intelligence (Edge Question)* (Harper Perennial, 2015), p. 164.
71.Haidt, *Happiness Hypothesis*, p. 50.
72.Robert Wright, *Why Buddhism Is True: The Science and Philosophy of Meditation and Enlightenment* (Simon & Schuster, 2017), p. 28.
73.Wright, *Why Buddhism Is True*, p. 7.
74.Wright, *Why Buddhism Is True*, p. 7.
75.Wright, *Why Buddhism Is True*, p. 8.
76.Wright, *Why Buddhism Is True*, p. 8.
77.Haidt, *Happiness Hypothesis*, p. 50.
78.Dormehl, *Thinking Machines*, p. 172.
79.Whybrow, *Well-Tuned Brain*, p. 62.
80.John Bargh, *Before You Know It: The Unconscious Reasons We Do What We Do* (Atria Books, 2017), p. 8.
81.Whybrow, *Well-Tuned Brain*, p. 62.
82.Haidt, *Happiness Hypothesis*, p. 140.
83.Wright, *Why Buddhism Is True*, p. 34.
84.Hawkins, *A Thousand Brains*, p. 96.

Chapter 6

85.Joseph LeDoux, *The Deep History of Ourselves: The Four Billion-Year Story of How We Got Conscious Brains* (Penguin Books, 2019), p. 179.
86.LeDoux, *Anxious*,
87.Bessel van der Kolk, *The Body Keeps the Score: Brain, Mind, and Body in the Healing of Trauma* (Penguin Books, 2014), p. 124.
88.Fabritius and Hagemann, *Leading Brain*, p. 50.
89.van der Kolk, *Body Keeps the Score*, p. 124.

90.Antonio Damasio, *Feeling & Knowing: Making Minds Conscious* (Pantheon, 2021), p. 76.
91.Brockman, ed., *What to Think About Machines That Think*, p. 37.
92.Norman Doidge, *The Brain's Way of Healing: Remarkable Discoveries and Recoveries from the Frontiers of Neuroplasticity* (Penguin Life, 2015), p. 65.
93.Haidt, *Happiness Hypothesis*, p. 196.
94.Ben Johnson, *The Healing Code: 6 Minutes to Heal the Source of Your Health, Success, or Relationship Issue* (Balance, 2011), p. 44.

Chapter 7

95.Daniel J. Levitin, The Organized Mind: Thinking Straight in the Age of Information Overload (Allen Lane, 2014), loc. 3286.
96.Hawkins, *A Thousand Brains*, p. 28.
97.LeDoux, *Anxious*, p. 85.
98.Sarah Peyton, *Your Resonant Self: Guided Meditations and Exercises to Engage Your Brain's Capacity for Healing* (W. W. Norton, 2017), p. 8.
99.Rick Hanson, *Neurodharma: New Science, Ancient Wisdom, and Seven Practices of the Highest Happiness* (Harmony, 2020), p. 195.
100.Daniel G. Amen, *Change Your Brain, Change Your Life (Revised and Expanded)* (Harmony, 2015), p. 90.
101.Kristen Willeumier, *Biohack Your Brain: How to Boost Cognitive Health, Performance & Power* (William Morrow, 2020), p. 11.
102.Doidge, *Brain's Way of Healing*, p. 58.
103.Willeumier, *Biohack Your Brain*, p. 11.
104.Bernard Zalc and Florence Rosier, *Myelin: The Brain's Supercharger* (Oxford University Press, 2018), p. 43.
105.Willeumier, *Biohack Your Brain*, p. 35.
106.Willeumier, *Biohack Your Brain*, p. 35.
107.LeDoux, *Synaptic Self*, p. 179.
108.Jeff Brown and Mark Fenske, *The Winner's Brain: 8 Strategies Great Minds Use to Achieve Success* (Da Capo Lifelong Books, 2010), p.162
109.Leonard Mlodinow, *Elastic: Unlocking Your Brain's Ability to Embrace Change* (Vintage, 2018), p. 180.
110.LeDoux, *Deep History of Ourselves*, p. 249.
111.Brewer, *Craving Mind*, p. 86.

112.Mlodinow, *Elastic*, p. 181.

113.Iain McGilchrist, *The Master and His Emissary: The Divided Brain and the Making of the Western World* (Yale University Press, 2019), p. 33.

114.Nick D. Dingman, *Your Brain, Explained: What Neuroscience Reveals About Your Brain and Its Quirks* (Nicholas Brealey, 2019), p.20

115.Whybrow, *Well-Tuned Brain*, p. 93.

116.Dingman, *Your Brain, Explained*, p. 20.

Chapter 8

117.LeDoux, *Synaptic Self*, p. 149.

118.LeDoux, *Synaptic Self*, p. 206.

119.Rick Hanson, *Hardwiring Happiness: The New Brain Science of Contentment, Calm, and Confidence* (Harmony, 2013), p. 21.

120.Faith G. Harper, *Unfuck Your Brain: Using Science to Get Over Anxiety, Depression, Anger, Freak-outs, and Triggers* (Microcosm Publishing, 2017), p. 18.

121.Peyton, *Your Resonant Self*, p. 157.

122.LeDoux, *Synaptic Self*, p. 206.

123.Dingman, *Your Brain, Explained*, p. 19.

124.LeDoux, *Synaptic Self*, p. 7.

125.LeDoux, *Anxious*, p. 37.

126.LeDoux, *Anxious*, p. 145.

127.LeDoux, *Deep History of Ourselves*, p. 350.

128.Ronald Siegel, *The Science of Mindfulness* (The Great Courses, 2014), p. 392.

129.Siegel, *Science of Mindfulness*, p. 392.
Hanson, *Neurodharma*, p. 31.

130.LeDoux, *Anxious*, p. 35.

131.LeDoux, *Anxious*, p. 89.

132.LeDoux, *Anxious*, p. 285.

133.Dingman, *Your Brain, Explained*, p. 20.

134.LeDoux, *Synaptic Self*, p. 7.

135.LeDoux, *Anxious*, p. 210.

136.LeDoux, *Synaptic Self*, p. 123.

137.LeDoux, *Anxious*, p. 210.

138.Willeumier, *Biohack Your Brain*, p. 36.

139.Daniel Goleman, *Emotional Intelligence: Why It Can Matter More Than IQ* (Bantam, 2012), p. 15.
140.Goleman, *Emotional Intelligence*, p. 12.
141.Goleman, *Emotional Intelligence*, p. 13.
142.LeDoux, *Deep History of Ourselves*, p. 218.
143.LeDoux, *Synaptic Self*, p. 121.
144.LeDoux, *Synaptic Self*, p. 123.
145.Goleman, *Emotional Intelligence*, p. 20.
146.LeDoux, *Anxious*, p. 213.
147.LeDoux, *Anxious*, p. 207.
148.Amen, *Change Your Brain, Change Your Life*, p. 95.
149.Ethan Kross, *Chatter: The Voice in Our Head, Why It Matters, and How to Harness It* (Crown, 2021), p. 39.
150.Fabritius and Hagemann, *Leading Brain*, p. 50.
151.LeDoux, *Anxious*, p. 58.
Kross, *Chatter*, p. 39.
152.LeDoux, *Synaptic Self*, p. 39.
153.Hermann Hesse, *Siddhartha's Brain: Unlocking the Ancient Science of Enlightenment* (Mariner Books, 2016), loc. 639.
154.Fabritius and Hagemann, *Leading Brain*, p. 35.
155.Daniel J. Levitin, *Successful Aging: A Neuroscientist Explores the Power and Potential of Our Lives* (Allen Lane, 2020), p. 154.
156.Levitin, *Successful Aging*, p. 156.
157.Peyton, *Your Resonant Self*, p. 154.
158.Levitin, *Successful Aging*, p. 156.
159.Levitin, *Successful Aging*, p. 156.
160.Siegel, *Science of Mindfulness*, p. 392.
161.Willeumier, *Biohack Your Brain*, p. 15.
162.Siegel, *Science of Mindfulness*, p. 392.
163.Hanson, *Neurodharma*, p. 61.
164.Doidge, *Brain's Way of Healing*, p. 111.

Chapter 9

165.Lipton, *Biology of Belief*, p. 173.
166.Fabritius and Hagemann, *Leading Brain*, p. 156.
167.Moshe Bar, *Mindwandering* (Hachette Go, 2022.), p. 89.
168.Whybrow, *Well-Tuned Brain*, p. 61.
169.Whybrow, *Well-Tuned Brain*, p. 7.

170.Yates et al., *Mind Illuminated*, p. 345.
171.Doidge, *Brain's Way of Healing*, p. 59.
172.Whybrow, *Well-Tuned Brain*, p. 58.
173.Whybrow, *Well-Tuned Brain*, p. 60.
174.Whybrow, *Well-Tuned Brain*, p. 58.
175.Whybrow, *Well-Tuned Brain*, p. 7.
176.Daniel J. Siegel, *Aware: The Science and Practice of Presence—The Groundbreaking Meditation Practice* (TarcherPerigee, 2018), p.19
177.Yates et al., *Mind Illuminated*, p. 345.
178.Doidge, *Brain's Way of Healing*, p. 59.

Chapter 10

179.Levitin, *Organized Mind*, loc. 991.
180.Levitin, *Successful Aging*, p. 79.
181.Levitin, *Successful Aging*, p. 79.
182.Levitin, *Organized Mind*, loc. 991.
183.Levitin, *Organized Mind*, loc. 1004.
184.Peyton, *Your Resonant Self*, p. 13.
185.Hesse, *Siddhartha's Brain*, loc. 1687.
186.Levitin, *Organized Mind*, loc. 991.
187.Siegel, *Aware*, p. 138.
188.Bar, *Mindwandering*, p. 212.
189.Siegel, *Science of Mindfulness*, p. 494.
190.Hesse, *Siddhartha's Brain*, loc. 378.
191.Hesse, *Siddhartha's Brain*, loc. 393.
192.Harris, *Waking Up*, p. 119.
193.Peyton, *Your Resonant Self*, p. 17.
194.Gabor Maté, *In the Realm of Hungry Ghosts* (Knopf Canada, 2009), p. 185.
195.Maté, *In the Realm of Hungry Ghosts*, p. 187.
196.Peyton, *Your Resonant Self*, p. 17.
197.Hanson, *Neurodharma*, p. 125.
198.Siegel, *Aware*, p. 144.

Chapter 11

199.Brockman, ed., *What to Think About Machines That Think*, p. 313

200.Sternberg, *Neurologic*, p. 58.
201.Kross, *Chatter*, p. 27.
202.LeDoux, *Anxious*, p. 149.
203.Mlodinow, *Elastic*, p. 84.
204.Hanson, *Hardwiring Happiness*, p. 42.
205.Scott Kaufman, *Ungifted* (Basic Books, 2013), p. 199.
206.Mlodinow, *Elastic*, p. 181.
207.LeDoux, *Deep History of Ourselves*, p. 249.
208.LeDoux, *Synaptic Self*, p. 318.
209.LeDoux, *Synaptic Self*, p. 319.
210.Mlodinow, *Elastic*, p. 180.
211.Mlodinow, *Elastic*, p. 83.
212.LeDoux, *Anxious*, p. 207.
213.LeDoux, *Synaptic Self*, p. 176.
214.David Rock, *Quiet Leadership: Six Steps to Transforming Performance at Work* (HarperCollins e-books, 2009), p. 233.
215.Daniel Bor, *The Ravenous Brain* (Basic Books, 2012), p. 188.
216.LeDoux, *Anxious*, p. 158.
217.Fabritius and Hagemann, *Leading Brain*, p. 71.
218.Whybrow, *Well-Tuned Brain*, p. 96.
219.LeDoux, *Deep History of Ourselves*, p. 225.
220.LeDoux, *Synaptic Self*, p. 318.
221.LeDoux, *Synaptic Self*, p. 192.
222.LeDoux, *Anxious*, p. 158.
223.LeDoux, *Anxious*, p. 223.
224.LeDoux, *Anxious*, p. 223.
225.LeDoux, *Anxious*, p. 158.
226.Kaufman, *Ungifted*, p. 200.
227.LeDoux, *Synaptic Self*, p. 176.
228.Kaufman, *Ungifted*, p. 200.
229.LeDoux, *Anxious*, p. 177.
230.Levitin, *Organized Mind*, loc. 1045.
231.Levitin, *Organized Mind*, loc. 449.
232.Levitin, *Organized Mind*, loc. 627.
233.Levitin, *Organized Mind*, loc. 627.
234.LeDoux, *Deep History of Ourselves*, loc. 142.
235.Levitin, *Organized Mind*, loc. 1004.
236.Nina Kraus, *Of Sound Mind* (The MIT Press, 2021.), p. 67.

Chapter 12

237.Joe Dispenza, *Breaking the Habit of Being Yourself: How to Lose Your Mind and Create a New One* (Hay House, 2012), p. 57.
238.Bargh, *Before You Know It*, p. 250.
239.Freddy Jacquin, *Hypnotherapy* (2024), loc. 1933.
240.Dispenza, *Breaking the Habit*, p. 57.
241.van der Kolk, *Body Keeps the Score*, p. 388.
242.Kelly Noonan Gores, *Heal* (Atria Books/Beyond Words 2019.), p. 44.
243.Hawkins, *A Thousand Brains*, p. 48.
244.Brown and Fenske, *Winner's Brain*, p. 160.
245.Peter Attia, *Outlive: The Science and Art of Longevity* (Harmony, 2023), p. 272.
246.van der Kolk, *Body Keeps the Score*, p. 388.
247.Hanson, *Neurodharma*, p. 61.
248.Goleman, *Focus*, p. 197.
249.Doidge, *Brain's Way of Healing*, p. 228.
250.Hanson, *Neurodharma*, p. 61.
251.LeDoux, *Anxious*, p. 313.

Chapter 14

252.Jeffrey Brantley, *Calming Your Anxious Mind: How Mindfulness and Compassion Can Free You from Anxiety, Fear, and Panic* (New Harbinger Publications, 2007), p. 59.
253.Jon Kabat-Zinn, *Wherever You Go, There You Are* (Hachette Books, 2010), p. 82.
254.Noonan Gores, *Heal*, p. 158.
255.Johnson, *Healing Code*, p. 281.
256.Thich Nhat Hanh, *The Art of Power* (HarperOne, 2009), p. 177.
257.Hesse, *Siddhartha's Brain*, loc. 781.
258.Siegel, *Aware*, p. 48.
259.Christopher Germer, *The Mindful Path to Self-Compassion* (The Guilford Press, 2009), p. 43.
260.Germer, *Mindful Path to Self-Compassion* (The Guilford Press, 2009), p. 43.
261.Thich Nhat Hanh, *Happiness: Essential Mindfulness Practices* (Parallax Press, 2005), p. 5.

262.Hanh, *Happiness*, p. 3.
263.Hesse, *Siddhartha's Brain*, loc. 781.
264.Hanh, *Art of Power*, p. 177.
265.Siegel, *Science of Mindfulness*, p. 103.
266.Hesse, *Siddhartha's Brain*, loc. 781.
267.Harper, *Unfuck Your Brain*, p. 69.
268.Johnson, *Healing Code*, p. 282.
269.Harris, *Waking Up*, p. 122.
270.Jackson MacKenzie, *Whole Again* (TarcherPerigee, 2009.), p. 3.
271.Siegel, *Science of Mindfulness*, p. 115.
272.van der Kolk, *Body Keeps the Score*, p. 306.
273.Kabat-Zinn, *Wherever You Go, There You Are*, p. 18.
274.Mlodinow, *Elastic*, p. 36.

Chapter 15

275.Hanh, Happiness, p.10.
276.Thich Nhat Hanh, *The Miracle of Mindfulness: An Introduction to the Practice of Meditation* (Beacon Press, 1996), p. 27.
277.Bal Pawa, *The Mind-Body Cure: Heal Your Pain, Anxiety, and Fatigue by Controlling Chronic Stress* (Greystone Books, 2020), p.254
278.Hanh, *Happiness*, p. 4.
279.James A. Afremow, *The Champion's Mind* (Rodale Books, 2015), p. 173.
280.Thich Nhat Hanh, *The Heart of the Buddha's Teaching: Transforming Suffering into Peace, Joy, and Liberation* (Harmony, 2015), p. 70.
281.Harper, *Unfuck Your Brain*, p. 67.
282.Goleman, *Focus*, p. 51.
283.Jon Kabat-Zinn, *Full Catastrophe Living (Revised Edition): Using the Wisdom of Your Body and Mind to Face Stress, Pain, and Illness* (Bantam, 2013), p. 65.
284.Jon Kabat-Zinn, *Falling Awake: How to Practice Mindfulness in Everyday Life* (Hachette Books, 2018), p. 112.
285.Pema Chödrön, *How to Meditate: A Practical Guide to Making Friends with Your Mind* (Sounds True, 2013), p. 108.
286.Chödrön, *How to Meditate*, p. 108.
287.Kabat-Zinn, *Full Catastrophe Living*, p. 65.

288.Kabat-Zinn, *Falling Awake*, p. 114.
289.Wright, *Why Buddhism Is True*, p. 21.
290.Hanh, *Miracle of Mindfulness*, p. 58.
291.Hanh, *Miracle of Mindfulness*, p. 58.
292.Hanh, *Miracle of Mindfulness*, p. 39.

Chapter 16

293.Hawkins, *A Thousand Brains*, p. 14.
294.Willeumier, *Biohack Your Brain*, p. 38.
295.Indre Viskontas, *Brain Myths Exploded: Lessons from Neuroscience* (The Great Courses, 2017), p. 19.
296.Mark Humphries, *The Spike: An Epic Journey Through the Brain in 2.1 Seconds* (Princeton University Press, 2021), p. 161.
297.Zalc and Rosier, *Myelin*, p. 87.
298.Jacquin, *Hypnotherapy*, loc. 1933.
299.Hawkins, *A Thousand Brains*, p. 54.
300.Zalc and Rosier, *Myelin*, p. 31.
301.Zalc and Rosier, *Myelin*, p. 31.
302.Doidge, *Brain's Way of Healing*, p. 97.
303.Joe Dispenza, *Evolve Your Brain: The Science of Changing Your Mind* (Health Communications, 2010), p. 82.
304.Jacquin, *Hypnotherapy*, loc. 1933.
305.Dispenza, *Evolve Your Brain*, p. 79.
306.Zalc and Rosier, *Myelin*, p. 1.
307.Dispenza, *Evolve Your Brain*, p. 142.

Chapter 17

308.Viskontas, *Brain Myths Exploded*, p. 19.
309.Zalc and Rosier, *Myelin*, p. 37.
310.Zalc and Rosier, *Myelin*, p. 58.
311.Zalc and Rosier, *Myelin*, p. 71.
312.Daniel Coyle, *The Talent Code: Greatness Isn't Born. It's Grown. Here's How* (Bantam, 2009), p. 48.
313.Coyle, *Talent Code*, p. 38.
314.Zalc and Rosier, *Myelin*, p. 70.
315.Whybrow, *Well-Tuned Brain*, p. 99.
316.Coyle, *Talent Code*, p. 40.

Chapter 18

317.Humphries, The Spike, p. 2.

318.LeDoux, *Deep History of Ourselves*, p. 180.

319.Susanne Foitzik and Olaf Fritsche, *Planet of the Ants: The Hidden Worlds and Extraordinary Lives of Earth's Tiny Conquerors* (The Experiment, 2022), p.105

320.Mlodinow, *Elastic*, p. 80.

321.Mlodinow, *Elastic*, p. 80.

322.Mlodinow, *Elastic*, p. 82.

323.Dispenza, *Evolve Your Brain*, p. 142.

324.Som Bathla, *Think With Full Brain* (2019), p. 39.

Chapter 19

325.Brockman, ed., What to Think About Machines That Think, p.12

326.Richard Yonck, *Heart of the Machine: Our Future in a World of Artificial Emotional Intelligence* (Arcade, 2017), p. 66.

327.Yonck, *Heart of the Machine*, p. 66.

328.Dormehl, *Thinking Machines*, p. 50.

329.Susan Schneider, *Artificial You: AI and the Future of Your Mind* (Princeton University Press, 2019), p. 11.

330.Wooldridge, *Brief History of Artificial Intelligence*, p. 119.

Chapter 20

331.Shane, *You Look Like a Thing*, p. 8.

332.Wooldridge, *Brief History of Artificial Intelligence*, p. 16.

333.Wooldridge, *Brief History of Artificial Intelligence*, p. 16.

334.Shane, *You Look Like a Thing*, p. 22.

335.du Sautoy, *Creativity Code*, p. 24.

336.Shane, *You Look Like a Thing*, p. 61.

337.Shane, You Look Like a Thing, p. 9.

Chapter 21

338.Humphries, *The Spike*, p. 161.

339.Hanson, *Hardwiring Happiness*, p. 18.

340.Norman Doidge, *The Brain That Changes Itself: Stories of Personal Triumph from the Frontiers of Brain Science* (Penguin Life, 2007), p. 293.

341.Rebecca Schwarzlose, *Brainscapes* (Mariner Books, 2021), p. 131.

342.Whybrow, *Well-Tuned Brain*, p. 203.

343.Whybrow, *Well-Tuned Brain*, p. 97.
344.Whybrow, *Well-Tuned Brain*, p. 97.
345.Brewer, *Craving Mind*, loc. 74.
346.Hanson, *Hardwiring Happiness*, p. 10.
347.Buonomano, *Brain Bugs*, p. 30.
348.Brewer, *Craving Mind*, loc. 87.
349.Mark Wolynn, *It Didn't Start with You: How Inherited Family Trauma Shapes Who We Are and How to End the Cycle* (Penguin Life, 2016), p. 26.
350.Hawkins, *A Thousand Brains*, p. 205.
351.Schwarzlose, *Brainscapes*, p. 139.
352.Schwarzlose, *Brainscapes*, p. 140.
353.Schwarzlose, *Brainscapes*, p. 143.
354.Whybrow, *Well-Tuned Brain*, p. 60.

Chapter 22

355.Brewer, *Craving Mind*, loc. 87.
356.Francine Shapiro, *Getting Past Your Past: Take Control of Your Life with Self-Help Techniques from EMDR Therapy* (Rodale Books, 2013), p. 3.
357.Hawkins, *A Thousand Brains*, p. 54.
358.Bathla, *Think With Full Brain*, p. 44.
359.Coyle, *Talent Code*, p. 41.
360.Bor, *Ravenous Brain*, p. 106.
361.Hawkins, *A Thousand Brains*, p. 54.
362.Amen and Amen, *Brain Warrior's Way*, p. 187.
363.Wolynn, *It Didn't Start with You*, p. 49.
364.Bar, *Mindwandering*, p. 89.
365.Doidge, *Brain's Way of Healing*, p. 59.
366.Doidge, *Brain's Way of Healing*, p. 59.
367.Doidge, *Brain That Changes Itself*, p. 64.

Chapter 23

368.Eric R. Kandel, *The Disordered Mind: What Unusual Brains Tell Us About Ourselves* (Farrar, Straus and Giroux, 2018), p. 143.
369.Goleman, *Focus*, p. 164.
370.Malcolm Gladwell, *Outliers: The Story of Success* (Little, Brown, 2008), p. 40.

371.Gladwell, *Outliers*, p. 39.
372.Goleman, *Focus*, p. 162.
373.Gladwell, *Outliers*, p. 38.
374.Gladwell, *Outliers*, p. 38.
375.Kaufman, *Ungifted*, p. 161.
376.Kaufman, *Ungifted*, p. 162.
377.Kaufman, *Ungifted*, p. 162.
378.Geoff Colvin, *Talent Is Overrated* (Portfolio, 2008), p. 59.
379.Kaufman, *Ungifted*, p. 162.
380.Goleman, *Focus*, p. 162.
381.David Shenk, *The Genius in All of Us* (Anchor, 2010), loc. 908.
382.Goleman, *Focus*, p. 164.
383.Colvin, *Talent Is Overrated*, p. 67.
384.Daniel Coyle, *The Talent Code*, p. 44.
385.Daniel Coyle, *The Little Book of Talent* (Bantam, 2012), p. 50.
386.Coyle, *Little Book of Talent*, p. 21.
387.Coyle, *Little Book of Talent*, p. 21.
388.Coyle, *Talent Code*, p. 44.
389.Coyle, *Little Book of Talent*, p. 34.
390.Craig M. Wright, *The Hidden Habits of Genius: Beyond Talent, IQ, and Grit—Unlocking the Secrets of Greatness* (Dey Street Books, 2020), p. 50.
391.Shenk, *Genius in All of Us* (Anchor, 2010), p.35
392.Howard Gardner, *Five Minds for the Future* (Harvard Business Review Press, 2009), p. 83.
393.Colvin, *Talent Is Overrated* (Portfolio, 2008), p. 61.
394.Fabritius and Hagemann, *Leading Brain*, p. 254.
395.Shenk, *Genius in All of Us*, loc. 648.
396.George Leonard, *Mastery: The Keys to Success and Long-Term Fulfillment* (Plume, 1992), p. 5.
397.Ed Catmull and Amy Wallace, *Creativity, Inc.: Overcoming the Unseen Forces That Stand in the Way of True Inspiration* (Random House Canada, 2014), loc. 993.
398.Napoleon Hill, *Think and Grow Rich* (Sound Wisdom, 2019), p. 3.
399.Shenk, *Genius in All of Us*, p. 832.
400.Robert M. Sapolsky, *Behave* (Penguin Books, 2017), p. 152.

Chapter 24

401.Wolynn, *It Didn't Start with You*, p. 50.
402.Afremow, *Champion's Mind* (Rodale Books, 2015), p. 47.
403.Sternberg, *Neurologic*, p. 97.
404.Shapiro, *Getting Past Your Past*, p. 268.
405.Sternberg, *Neurologic*, p. 75.
406.Sternberg, *Neurologic*, p. 75.
407.Fabritius and Hagemann, *Leading Brain*, p. 180.
408.Sternberg, *Neurologic*, p. 78.
409.Brown and Fenske, *Winner's Brain*, p. 98.
410.Afremow, *Champion's Mind*, p. 48.
411.Sternberg, *Neurologic*, p. 76.
412.Bargh, *Before You Know It*, p. 248.
413.Afremow, *Champion's Mind*, p. 50.
414.Sternberg, *Neurologic*, p. 73.

Chapter 25

415.Scott Kaufman, *Intelligence Redefined* (Basic Books, 2013), p. 10.
416.Shenk, *Genius in All of Us*, p. 388.
417.Kaufman, *Ungifted*, p. 10.
418.Shenk, *Genius in All of Us*, loc. 231.
419.Shenk, *Genius in All of Us*, loc. 231.
420.Wright, *Hidden Habits of Genius*, p. 16.
421.Wright, *Hidden Habits of Genius*, p. 16.
422.Levitin, *Successful Aging*, p. 6.
423.Mlodinow, *Elastic*, p. 24.
424.Shenk, *Genius in All of Us*, loc. 241.
425.Fabritius and Hagemann, *Leading Brain*, p. 18.
426.Levitin, *Successful Aging*, p. 6.
427.Shenk, *Genius in All of Us*, loc. 249.
428.Myers, *How Do We Know Ourselves?*, p. 159.
429.Shenk, *Genius in All of Us*, loc. 388.

About the Author

Alan Bodnar is an emerging neurophilosopher, researcher, and founder of *The Self-Driving You*. For the past decade, Alan has worked to translate complex science into a self-guided framework that allows people to get back in the driver's seat of their mind and to take control of automatic responses. Alan's project started as an attempt to reverse-engineer his own wiring and test what works in real life. His work is focused on clear strategies, measurable practice, and evidence that holds up when the rubber meets the road.

www.ingramcontent.com/pod-product-compliance
Lightning Source LLC
LaVergne TN
LVHW091149080826
845145LV00008B/2309

* 9 7 8 1 0 6 9 9 8 3 1 3 8 *